Mad or Bad

To those whose minds were opened before me

Mad or Bad

Crime and Insanity in Victorian Britain

David J. Vaughan

PEN & SWORD
HISTORY

First published in Great Britain in 2017 by
Pen & Sword History
an imprint of
Pen & Sword Books Ltd
47 Church Street
Barnsley
South Yorkshire
S70 2AS

ISBN 978 1 47386 413 9

A CIP catalogue record for this book is available from the British
Library

Typeset in Ehrhardt by
Mac Style Ltd, Bridlington, East Yorkshire
Printed and bound in the UK by CPI Group (UK) Ltd,
Croydon, CRO 4YY

Pen & Sword Books Ltd incorporates the imprints of Pen & Sword
Archaeology, Atlas, Aviation, Battleground, Discovery, Family
History, History, Maritime, Military, Naval, Politics, Railways, Select,
Transport, True Crime, and Fiction, Frontline Books, Leo Cooper,
Praetorian Press, Seaforth Publishing and Wharncliffe.

For a complete list of Pen & Sword titles please contact
PEN & SWORD BOOKS LIMITED
47 Church Street, Barnsley, South Yorkshire, S70 2AS, England
E-mail: enquiries@pen-and-sword.co.uk
Website: www.pen-and-sword.co.uk

Contents

Acknowledgements

So many people have made this book happen ...

There are those long-since gone – men, women and children – who gave both their reputations *and* lives to the insanity cause. Thank you all for the legacy you left us.

In the present, there are too many to mention, but some deserve credit for their unstinting support. The unsung heroes who look after our archives, including court records, asylum case notes, newspaper cuttings and Parliamentary laws. Often managed by local authorities, their efforts and patience have made this book what it is – in particular: Steven Hobbs (Wiltshire & Swindon), Mark Stevens (West Berkshire), Chris Low and Will Phillips (Buckinghamshire, *Centre for Studies* and *Museum*, respectively), Andrew Lott (London Metropolitan), Helen Wicker (Kent) and numerous more.

Heartfelt thanks also to Cate Hopkins at Amgueddfa Cymru (National Museum Wales) Katie Amos and Ann Smith (Reading Borough Libraries) and Sharon Howard (*Old Bailey Proceedings Online*).

To all image providers* – including Wellcome Library, London; British Library; Amgueddfa Cymru; and the many Local Studies collections with which this country is blessed (see bibliography).

But mostly to *you*, for your thirst for the subject – many, I know, will subscribe to my ongoing blog (http://criminalunacy.blogspot.co.uk). Numbers and comments have encouraged the author, to further his passion and in all that he does.

To all – I hope you enjoy these simple fruits of my labours.

---

* All efforts have been made to respect copyright issues. Any oversights were made without malice aforethought or evil intent.

Introduction

'The possible increase in acquittals owing to insanity, the possible role of the insanity plea in encouraging murder, and the effect of commuting capital cases because of insanity, were therefore natural topics for judicial and journalistic alarm.' (Blackwell 1844 in Smith 1981a: 29)

This book is about people. Those standing trial, those furthering progress, the compassionate few and those empowered to judge. For as long as there are people, there is punishment and crime.

In Victorian Britain, another issue arose: *was the defendant in control of their mind?*

In an era with the sentence of death, resolving this quandary was a matter of life.

From within this morass came medico-legal debates – two points of view, destined to clash. The medic – the *alienist* – who saw exculpation in madness; and the law, rejecting it all as an easy escape.

The truth, as so often, lay somewhere between …

Though this is not an academic treatise – it avoids defining mental disorders or penal reform – it provides a brief introduction to a pertinent history and retells real-life cases like seldom before. In short: was the accused 'mad' or 'bad' when they committed their crime? And what then should be done with those considered insane?

Four short, prefatory chapters set out the background to the on-going debates:

Part 1, *Who's Who*, sets the scene through its major exponents: the alienists struggling with new diagnoses, striving for acceptance in the theatre of law; the Law itself – politicians, judges, and counsel – questioning the premise of fairness for all. Those outside the courts – the public and press – who looked on in horror as battle commenced. And the jury – who experienced the toughest dilemma – unqualified, inexperienced yet determining life.

Part 2, *Insanity Conditions*, highlights the maladies that formed the insanity plea. Though often rejected, at least by the lawyers, these redefined 'ailments' brought hope to the few.

Part 3, *History of Debate*, glances back at the moments the subject took shape. From Hadfield and Oxford, and definitive trials, to Daniel M'Naghten and his 'lucky' escape. From these came the Rules – *the* point of reference – when exploring the impact of the insanity plea.

Part 4, *Mad Women, Bad Women* – a chapter necessarily short – casts an eye on the issues that deserve their own book. From hysteria to neurasthenia, 'monthly madness' to birth, women suffered conditions 'accepted' by many yet defined by the few. *Male-centric* 'solutions' that brought not only horror but, perversely, some hope in this clinical world. For who, other than women, felt the double-edged sword: receiving both terror and favour for their criminal deeds?

Finally, in Part 5, *Case Histories*, produces the main part of the book – some twenty-five real-life accounts of the struggles in court. Each drawn from different parts of the country – from Wales to Scotland, north-east England, down to the south – all are defined by three essential provisions: alleged crime, insanity condition and an outcome in court. [In many, what happened after will leave you amazed!]

By the end, there remains one final dilemma: did mad people suffer, or the guilty escape? This I leave for the reader to fathom, though no such assessment is needed at all. The book – the case histories especially – holds plenty of interest and all of it true.

To this I commend not just the writing, but the lives loved and lost through the insanity plea.

Caveat All details have been scrupulously researched and no interpretations attempted. I offer no diagnoses or opinion of fact. All speech is repeated as it appeared in the records; and textual references are given throughout. I apologise for any errors or omissions unwittingly suffered, which I hope won't detract from the enjoyment of this book.

More information is available at *criminalunacy.blogspot.co.uk* or via the author's website *davidjvaughan.co.uk*

Glossary of Terms

As appear in the book:

Assizes – county trials of more serious crimes, held usually at regular intervals (eg Spring, Summer etc)

Assoilzied Simpliciter – in Scotland, discharged free of guilt; no case to answer

'Bloody Code' – well established in eighteenth century Britain, listing nearly *three hundred* criminal offences punishable by death; by mid-nineteenth century, reduced to just three: murder, attempted murder and treason. High Treason – the last to survive – was eventually abolished by the Crime and Disorder Act (1998)

Burden of Proof – responsibility to establish the accused's 'fitness to plead' (see *Unfit to Plead* and *Insane on Arraignment*); oscillated between defence and prosecution counsel. [*See Part 5* for exemplary cases: Pritchard (1836), Davies the Elder (1853), Turton (1854)]

Commissioners in Lunacy – established in 1845 (*see Appendix 1*), to oversee the new county and private asylums (excluding Bethlem) and the general welfare of those found insane. Eleven in number plus secretary made twelve. Incipient holders included James Cowles Prichard (*see Part 1*) and Robert Skeffington Lutwidge (Secretary), Lewis Carroll's favourite uncle, murdered by an inmate at Fisherton House

Commutation – 'lessening' the sentence (eg from death to transportation or penal servitude for life). Frequently employed via the *Home Secretary's Mercy*

'**Diet Simpliciter**' – in Scotland, (*diet*) a meeting in court involving prosecution; (*simpliciter*) absolved of the charge

Diminished Responsibility – legal definition, latterly synonymous with the insanity plea. Introduced in England and Wales by 1960s, though accepted in Scotland a century before

Double Jeopardy – a legal inability to face the same charge again (eg having been tried but acquitted, say '*on the ground of insanity*'). Compare *Insane on Arraignment*

Her (His) Majesty's Pleasure – an indeterminate period (of incarceration), typically following an insanity plea. Often used while awaiting the *Home Secretary's Mercy*; though in rare cases, used until no longer *Unfit to Plead* (eg *see Pritchard & Turton, Part 5*). Enacted after Hadfield's trial (1800) (*see Part 3*)

Home Secretary's Mercy – power given to the Secretary of State to commute a more serious sentence (replaced Her (His) Majesty's Mercy from 1837 (1 Vict., c. 77))

Insane on Arraignment – when the accused is considered *either Unfit to Plead or* unable to grasp proceedings in Court [though they were not necessarily mad at the time of the crime]. Rarely was the trial heard, even when they were considered 'recovered' (but *see Turton, Part 5* for a case where it did)

'**Not Guilty on the Ground of Insanity**' – 'special verdict' brought in after Hadfield's trial (*see Part 3*), leading to the accused being detained at *Her Majesty's Pleasure*. If, subsequently, they were considered recovered, they were simply released – not made to stand trial again (see *Double Jeopardy*)

Pannel – the defendant in Scotland

Pardon – generic term, conveying Her (His) Majesty's 'intention' to remit a criminal sentence

Quarter Sessions – county-level hearings held each quarter (eg Lady Day, Michaelmas, etc) in cases of misdemeanour (more serious felonies were usually tried at *Assizes*)

Respite – when the sentence of death was *delayed* while under review. Revised in the latter part of the nineteenth century to '*respited until further signification of Her Majesty's Pleasure*'

'Right-Wrong Test' – (often) subjective test for the 'presence' of madness. Underpinned the Rules when insisting the accused was able to determine what they did was legally or morally wrong (*see Appendix 3*)

The Rules – major point of reference in the history of the insanity plea (*see Appendix 3*)

'Ticket of Leave' – administrative function allowing prisoners to re-enter society, having completed their sentence

Unfit to Plead – when the accused is unable to enter their plea. Often led to *Insane on Arraignment*; while in earlier cases, often referred to their being 'a mute' (eg *see Pritchard, Part 5*)

Chapter 1

Who's Who

Without people, this book would not be. Those accused gave the subject its innate human story. So too, the alienists, lawyers, politicians – and juries – of whom so few can here be named. To them all, however, we owe an unimpeachable debt.

Caveats: not considered exhaustive; author's interpretations using various sources; *highlighted* cases appear in *Part 5*

Alienists

> '*Psychiatrists who assesses the competence of a defendant in a law court*' (based on OED). Promoted the insanity plea in criminal trials, though not always present in court. Their work, reputations and public personae shaped the future of crime and insanity.

Those mentioned in the following pages:

John Charles Bucknill (Superintendent Devon Asylum) – maverick, commentator and lunacy reformer. Supported – and vexed – both sides in the crime and insanity wrangle. Rare success from the county (public) lunacy network, helped professionalise a discipline which he so often graced. His *Manual of Psychological Medicine* (1858) – co-authored with Daniel Hack Tuke – became the practitioner's 'bible'.

Thomas Clouston (Superintendent, Royal Morningside Asylum) – feared women's latent mental capacity and exhaustion from 'excessive' use of the mind. Supported *Fraser* in his 'sleep-walking' trial.

John Conolly – iconic exponent of 'moral management' and the end of restraint in lunacy care. Struggled to grasp insanity *causes* (eg see Conolly 1830), believing women more susceptible to damage than men. Cited the 'disruptive influences' of menstruation, motherhood and reproduction.

James George Davey (Medical Superintendent, Northwoods Asylum) – believed in the natural order of things. Diagnosed *unnatural* madness through a phrenological approach (van Whye n.d.). Much criticised witness in case of *James Pownall*.

William Charles Hood (Medical Superintendent, Bethlem) – appeasing witness in the case of *James Pownall* and supporter of early photography of the photogenically mad (cf Morison, below).

Thomas Laycock (Lecturer and Physician to the Queen in Scotland) – believed in the duality of the physical brain and ethereal mind; also function and impact of the nervous system and its relation to action. His *Nervous Diseases of Women* (1840) emanated from a belief in *impulsive insanity* – blaming a fault in the brain for loss of the 'will' (*see Part 2*).

Henry Manning (Medical Superintendent, Laverstock Asylum, Salisbury) – expert witness in *Maclean's* trial for High Treason, through which he 'confirmed' the accused's *irresistible moral impulse* (cf discrete entries in *Part 2*).

Henry Maudsley (Superintendent, Manchester Royal Lunatic Asylum) – juggernaut of the alienist movement, author of many seminal works. Attracted criticism for his views on the menstrual cycle – and its debilitating effect on a woman's 'volatile mind'. Strident views on *puerperal insanity* and on controversial eugenics. A keen (if now unpopular) author, his *Sex in Mind and in Education* and *Responsibility in Mental Disease* were both tracts of their time (both pub. 1874). Married Ann, John Conolly's daughter.

Sir Alexander Morison (visiting physician to Bethlem) – early student of mental disease. Reviewed many significant trials (eg *Brixey*). Gained notoriety for his sketches (*The Physiognomy of Mental Diseases*), and his objection to Conolly's distaste for restraint (Showalter 1987: 46).

Henry Turnbull Pringle (Superintendent, Bridgend Asylum) – single-handedly perhaps influenced the outcome of *Collins'* trial, by suggesting the man had suffered aural illusions.

James Cowles Prichard (founding Commissioner in Lunacy) – '…the author of by far the best English work on insanity in his generation' and deviser of *moral insanity* (Tuke 1891: 1). Expanded the notion that a person's morality could be distinct from their intellectual reason, undermining the Rules and the 'right-wrong test' (*see Appendix 3*). His *irresistible impulse* (eg to murder) earned him the unflattering epithet, the 'homicidal orgasm'.

Isaac Ray (American medic) – powerful voice in changing public perception of the insanity condition. Commentator on medical jurisprudence and critical of 'the Rules' and the 'right-wrong test' (*see Appendix 3*).

C. Lockhart Robertson (Physician to Sussex County Asylum) – one-time editor of Bucknill's *Journal of Mental Science*, worked hard to unify the alienist movement (Smith 1981a: 13). Nevertheless, condemned jurists and alienists alike in the *Brixey* debacle.

George Savage (Chief Medical Officer, Bethlem) – infamously dismissed spiritualism as 'a girl with hysterical symptoms' (Green and Troup 1999: 311). Became confused in his reason during *Dyer's* indictment.

Edgar Sheppard (Medical Superintendent, Male Department, Colney Hatch) – appeared as expert in *Maclean's* trial for High Treason.

Professor Alfred Swaine Taylor (Professor of Medical Jurisprudence) – author of *Principles and Practice of Medical Jurisprudence* (1865), his colossus on forensic science for body and mind. Achieved universal respect for his dual grasp of both medicine and law.

Daniel Hack Tuke (great-grandson of York Retreat founder) – brought alienist knowledge to the reading public, eg as co-author with Bucknill of their veritable tome (*see above*). Showed interest (and expertise) in human automatism, including somnambulism and its role in murderous acts (eg *Fraser*). Married another of Conolly's daughters, Sophia Jane.

Sir John Batty Tuke (Superintendent, Fife and Kinross Asylum) – Commentator on *puerperal insanity* – its prevalence and its connections to salacity and sex.

William Tuke – like Conolly, a fanatic of 'moral management'. Combined teaching and guidance with compassion and care. Founded the Quaker-run York Retreat, in 1796, and over the years crusaded asylum reform.

Caleb Williams (Medical Superintendent, York Retreat) – alienist witness and chronicler of the great poisoning case of *William Dove*.

Forbes B. Winslow – 'personally responsible for the legal acceptance of the insanity plea' (Showalter 1987: 173). Exponent of physicalism (*see Part 2*), his opus *On the Preservation of the Health of Body and Mind* (1842) connected brain structure with emotional and 'real' behaviour. A 'celebrity' medic, attracting frequent controversy when appearing in court (eg *Brough*). Prolific writer, including *The Plea of Insanity in Criminal Cases* (1843); and when founder and editor of the *Journal of Psychological Medicine* (1848–1860).

Lyttleton F. Winslow – son of Forbes Winslow, in whose shadow he struggled. Infamously offered an 'identification' of Jack the Ripper, leading to the authorities' suspicion he was describing himself!

David Yellowlees (Superintendent, Gartnavel Asylum) – prosecution witness who helped shape the unusual verdict in *Fraser's* sleep-walking case.

Judges

The 'Wicked Barons' – grouped for their abhorrence of the insanity plea as much as their titles. Barons Alderson, Bramwell, Parke, Gurney and Rolfe – presiding judges in many insanity trials – often warned juries not to 'follow their heart'. Instead, reinforced the Rules and the 'right-wrong test:

Sir Edward Alderson – one of fifteen judges who 'authored' the Rules. Disliked medical witness and even textbook opinion, rejecting a Grand Jury's view that the accused was unfit to stand trial (Walker 1968: 169). Introduced the widely-held test for determining '*Insanity on Arraignment*' (eg *see Pritchard*).

George William Bramwell – despised the alienist argument, investing more trust in a lay jury's opinion. Insisted confirmed lunatics should face the harshest of penalties, as they had not the intellect to work out for themselves what they had done had been wrong (eg in Smith 1981a: 105). When confronted by a juror who thought the accused might have suffered an uncontrollable impulse, he retorted: 'That did not make the offence [any] the less murder' (*ibid*).

Sir John Gurney – '[A] good criminal lawyer, though not deeply learned, and was an independent and acute, but severe and somewhat harsh judge' (Oxford DNB, 11767). Described by Alfred Dymond (*see below*) as 'the sternest of modern judges' (1865: 138).

James Parke – ferociously opposed to exculpatory madness, insisting he would never accept the plea unless it met with the Rules (ie *delusions* and a lost sense of reason). Dismissed *moral insanity* as a 'dangerous innovation coming in with the present century' (in Smith 1981a: 117), and lamented that 'the excuse of an irresistible impulse coexisting with the full (?) possession of reason would justify any crime whatever' (Taylor 1865: 1100).

Robert Monsey Rolfe – provoked often ribald debates between *irresistible* and *unresisted* impulses – too often with devastating effect (eg *Allnutt*). Demonstrated compassion when suggesting that being *only just able* to determine the wrongness of crime could yet unmask the prisoner as mad.

Other judges – Not all were as resistant to the insanity plea. Those appearing in *Part 5* (Case Histories) are *broadly* divided here between the two opposite camps [in the author's opinion]:

Pro	Intermediate	Anti
Lord Alexander Cockburn	Lord David Boyle	Lord Campbell
Lord Coleridge	Lord Denman	Cresswell Cresswell
Charles Crompton	James Lord Moncreiff	William Erle
William Maule		James Fitzjames Stephen (formerly)
John Patteson		
James Fitzjames Stephen (latterly)		
John Vaughan		
Edward Vaughan Williams		
William Wightman		

Home Secretaries

Since 1837, and the accession of a 'naive 18-year-old queen', responsibility for hearing appeals against capital sentences was handed to the Home Secretary – with variable effect. The following cases (*Part 5*) produced surprising results:

Case	Home Secretary	Comment
William Allnutt	Sir George Grey Bt	*see below*[1]
Thomas Collins	H. H. Asquith	Future Liberal Prime Minister
Rebecca Turton	Sir George Grey Bt	*see below*[1]
Mary Gallop	Sir James Graham	'[T]he most merciless of Home Secretaries' (Dymond 1865: 138)
Celestina Sommer	Sir George Grey Bt	[1]Perhaps one of the most unpopular holders of office, not least for this case
Moses Hatto	3rd Viscount Palmerston	Not one for bending

Commissioners In Lunacy

The Lunacy Commission was a side dish to the main course of the 1845 Acts (*see Appendix 1*). Defined through the Lunatics Care and Treatment Act (8 & 9 Vict., c. 100), half of their salaried number were drawn from the law. [Six salaried, eleven in total plus secretary.] First commissioners included Britain's 'father' of moral insanity – James Cowles Prichard.

Religion

Local reverends and holders of diocesan office wont to be included in the insanity debates. Though members of the Lords, Britain's upper political chamber, few caught the eye of the public or the ear of the press:

Samuel Wilberforce, Bishop of Oxford – powerful voice for the abolition of capital punishment – at least its cessation as a public display

John Allen, Archdeacon of Salop – saw Biblical endorsement for the sentence of death

Reverend Malin, Vicar of Broadwindsor – 'a zealous advocate for the punishment of death'

Reverend John Davis, Ordinary (Chaplain) of Newgate Gaol – frequent opponent of the insanity plea

Others

Thomas Mayo (physician) – made strident attempts to deny alienists changing the law (Smith 1981a: 118) Particular opponent of Prichard's moral insanity (*see Part 2*).

Alfred Dymond (Secretary of the Society for the Abolition of Capital Punishment) – pestered Home Secretaries with memorials for clemency, frequently citing the insanity plea. His *Law on Its Trial* (1865) became a clarion call for those of like minds. Witnessed the end of hanging in public (1868); no doubt, on its own, with unsatisfied glee.

Prison Medical Officers – extraordinary feature that Prison MOs, with little or no training, often opined on the prisoner's mind. *Maclean's* and *Allnutt's* cases are noteworthy examples.

Alleged Lunatics' Friend Society – sought to protect those *considered* insane, particularly though not exclusively in cases of inheritance and fortune.

Chapter 2

Insanity Conditions

'Madness, or mania, is much varied in its modes, but is really one and the same in its nature'

(Aretæus in Bucknill & Tuke 1858: 77)

Attempting a nosology (classification) of insanity conditions brings only despair. To the alienists, however, it formed the basis of a burgeoning insanity plea.

Listed here in glossary style (for easy reference, for example as you read through *Part 5*), each was rejected or accepted according to trial. The Rules (*see Appendix 3*) demanded the presence of delusions, yet even they were no guarantee of final success.

Note: definitions not necessarily modern or currently accepted; cross-references in *italics*; cases **highlighted** appear in Part 5.

* * *

alcoholism – in an age struggling with the evils of drink, crimes committed under its effects (ie self-inflicted) were seldom forgiven in criminal law. Prolonged alcoholism with/out *Delirium Tremens* more often was, the accused alleged to have lost all sense of reason (eg *Cruse*).

automatism – to act without thought, though often treated as guilty (eg *Fraser's* case); its acceptance in Britain's insanity corpus came after Bucknill & Tuke(1858). Variously included *epilepsy*, hypnotism, mesmerism, *somnambulism*, drunkenness (cf *alcoholism*) etc – leading to distinction between physical and insane (non-physical) states (Walker 1968: 175).

catamenial madness – insanity arising from disordered menstrual cycle – dismissed by many as an 'easy way out' (eg *Brixey*). Often used with the *physicalist* argument.

delirium – in short, suffering delusions or a perversion of mind.

delirium tremens – 'the DTs' or 'the sweats' – caused by substance withdrawal, often inducing a form of psychosis. Remained a legal defence on the grounds that the accused abjugated *mens rea* – ie had lost their senses to drink, over a period of time (not short-term intoxication).

delusions – including here illusions and visual and aural hallucinations – especially long-term paranoia or imaginary slights. Frequently demanded in law to 'prove' someone insane (*see Appendix 3*).

dementia – when the sufferer loses their previous mental capacity, for example through age (cf *idiocy*).

depravity – popular means of condemning insane behaviour, as inexcusable acts brought on by moral decay. Prevalent in cases of *moral insanity*, *homicidal mania* and impulsive insanity (*irresistible impulse*).

derangement – generic term for describing those suffering a mental disorder.

diminished responsibility – legal term indicating a state of mind as exculpation for criminal behaviour. Not accepted in English law before 1960s (in Scotland, a century before).

dipsomania – see *Delirium Tremens*

epilepsy – alienist 'proof' of *automatism*, from its uncontrollable movements (convulsions), claimed to persist long after attack. Considered to complicate other insanity conditions (eg *irresistible impulse*), though history of fits often rejected as an exculpatory state.

erotomania – traditionally, manic love for, or of, a particular object, whether real or imagined; subsequently redefined to encompass all forms. Commonly associated with *hysteria*, yet distinct from nymphomania (both genders), which originated in the sexual organs not in the mind (Bucknill & Tuke 1858).

free will – *volition*, a near metaphysical concept, alienists conjectured its impairment rendered the accused irresponsible in law. Fierce debates focussed on its true definition – ie whether a person's self-control could be 'negatived' by an insanity condition.

GPI (General Paralysis of the Insane) – typical symptoms were impaired speech (as though drunk) and awkward physical movement. Associated with nineteenth century promiscuous living and syphilitic men.

hereditary insanity – frequent 'cause' of a person's insanity (though not their actual condition). Popular defence in criminal trials [as well as chancery courts (non-criminal *de lunatico inquirendo*)].

homicidal mania – controversial diagnosis for those 'driven' to kill; from an uncontrollable impulse taking control of the *will*. May include visions or aural hallucination ('voices'). Or, in cases (eg *Dove*), from a general *propensity* caused by 'a lifetime's abuse'. Defined by lack of motive, no attempt to escape and not infrequent attempts to take one's own life (see *suicidal mania*).

hysteria – 'characterised by fits, choking sensations, and mental aberrations – a disorder of women that some saw as a form of possession, and others viewed as … another illness brought on by the peculiarities of the female constitution' (Scull 2011: 14). Others have argued for its presence in men (eg Goodman 2014).

idiocy (idiotcy) – most extreme form of mental 'deficient', typically a result of some (often congenital) under-development, or physical trauma.

imbecility – differs from *idiocy* in the sufferer's ability to complete at least some of life's stations (eg dressing, eating, etc).

insanity on arraignment – when accused is declared 'unfit to plead' or 'unfit to stand trial' (as opposed to the insanity plea – insane when the crime was committed) – eg *Pritchard and Turton*; *see also Glossary*).

irresistible impulse – contentious explanation for uncontrollable insanity, often as a result of the erosion of *will*. Dismissed by many within the medico-legal debates; eg 'we should not hear any more of *irresistible impulse*' (Morison 1848: 457) – often with disagreeable outcomes (see also *moral insanity*).

mania – (general) 'raving madness' – when the passions are 'exalted'; frequently followed by violent attacks. Affects first the emotions, then the intellectual powers, and is often accompanied by *delusions* as well. [Not to be confused with the following conditions:– *erotomania*, *homicidal mania*, kleptomania, *monomania*, nymphomania, *pyromania*, *religious mania*, *suicidal mania*, and others.]

melancholia – acute or gradual degeneration of spirit. Emanates from depression, or a moment of shock (eg bereavement). Can join particular conditions, such as *moral insanity*.

mens rea – psychological and/or legal awareness when committing a crime (cf *free will*, *volitional insanity*).

monomania – state of insanity aroused by one topic, ie being 'mad on one point'. Differs to (general) mania by being a *partial* obsession, with a heightened sense of conviction (*see table, below*). Often accompanied by *delusions*.

moral insanity – degradation of the morals without a necessary loss of reason (cf 'right-wrong test' and the Rules – *see Appendix 3*). Joined (not always) by an *irresistible impulse* and/or damaged *free will*. Popularised by James Cowles Prichard, though distrusted by many in medicine and law.

partial insanity – periodic or subjective insanity, coming in waves or from triggered attacks. Lockhart Robertson, like many, placed it between (general) *mania* and *idiocy/dementia*; but, unlike some, included *monomania*, *moral insanity* and instinctive insanity (eg *irresistible impulse*).

Monomania	Moral Insanity	Instinctive Insanity
Intellectual faculties disordered, a delusion present.	Intellectual faculties sound.	Intellectual faculties sound.
Generally diseased action of the moral principle, evinced by alteration of character, affections, or desires prior to the manifestation of the delusion and to the commission of crime.	Consists in diseased action of the moral principle, evinced by alteration of character, affections, or desires manifested prior to commission of crime.	Moral principle healthy, perfect consciousness of right and wrong, and of the extent of guilt, legally and morally incurred by the commission of crime.
Volition healthy, i.e. guided by the existing state of the reason and of the moral principle.	Volition healthy, i.e. guided by the existing state of the reason and of the moral principle.	Volition diseased; crime committed in opposition to the dictates of the reason and of the moral principle.

Partial Insanity (after Lockhart Robertson 1847)

physicalism – insanity connected to physical defects – in the nervous system, including the brain (eg Laycock's 'reflex function' (1845)). Allowed alienists to appropriate science ... and garner acceptance when appearing in court. Gave credence, in some quarters, to controversial *phrenology*.

phrenology – contended notion that the brain (and thus mind) may be divided in zones, each controlling particular moods or emotions.

physiognomy – diagnosis of insanity conditions from the patient's physical appearance (eg Morison 1843). Related to extreme cases of 'insanity management' through anatomical 'adjustment' (eg labiaplasty, clitoridectomy, etc).

puerperal insanity – affliction regarded as *the* curse of new Victorian mothers. Gave rise to other conditions: *mania, delusions, melancholia, dementia. See Part 4.*

pyromania – with or without motive (though often revenge) – a consequence of *moral insanity*. High incidence seen in pre-pubescent females.

religious mania – with or without *melancholia* or *delusions*. Typical cases include the accused's belief he/she was the Devil or deemed unworthy of God.

somnambulism – sleep-walking, incorporating any activity thus undertaken, whether felonious or not. History of contentious acceptance/rejection in law (eg *Fraser*).

suicidal mania – accompanied by *delusions* (eg imagined poverty), *melancholia* and/or some *irresistible* urge (cf *homicidal mania*, often its partner). Frequently seen when murder was committed in an effort to get hanged.

volitional insanity – exculpatory condition when *free will* is usurped by an insanity condition (cf *physicalism*).

Chapter 3

History of Debate

In this necessarily brief and staccato introduction to nineteenth century debate, several key milestones helped shape its future. When crime met madness and the insanity plea.

History

Once Hadfield (1800) and Oxford (1840) both 'escaped justice' – each on account of an imperfect mind – *crime and insanity* were never the same. By the time M'Naghten (1843) was acquitted 'on the ground of insanity' – using a term introduced after Hadfield's escape – the law *and* the public were voicing their fears: the dangers of unrestrained 'madmen' were simply too great.

[For details of M'Naghten's case, see Smith 1981a, Walker 1968 etc]

The Rules ...

In a Lords Committee set up almost as soon as M'Naghten stepped down [from the dock], fifteen of the nation's most eminent judges* considered the questions the peers had set (*see Appendix 3*). At their heart, a demand for a defendant's *delusions* (*see Part 2*) – meaning no other condition would be accepted in court.

In unseemly divisions, the Rules were laid down and with them a (re-defined) standard: had the accused known what they did was morally and/or legally wrong? This 'right-wrong test' undermined alienist reason: that the insane failed to *resist* an act they *knew* to be wrong.

---

* At least one, Justice Maule (*see Part 2*), objected to their 'one size fits all' (Smith 1981a: 15).

... Bring Utter Confusion

Their intractable wording brought utter confusion; and the jury especially shouldered the blame. Verdicts neglected legal opinion, while many considered they came from the heart.

Among the many, Harrington Tuke was a particular critic:

'[T]he power [to distinguish] between right and wrong exists frequently among those who are undoubtedly insane...' (in Walker 1968: 105).

While even James Fitzjames Stephen, the jurist and once their staunchest supporter, came to question their virtue having seen them applied. His report, some years later, to a Royal Commission, argued that a killer's awareness of the wrongness of murder:

'might [yet] be prevented from "controlling his...conduct"', in spite of his mind (in Smith 1981a: 79).

Only fourteen years into their uncertain existence, Bucknill rejected the Rules as outmoded and lame. And dismissed judges who:

'insisted upon the old delusion and consciousness of [the] right and wrong test' (1857: [94]).

Earlier still, Caleb Williams had openly stated that:

'whether the individual had a consciousness of right and wrong at the time he committed the particular act ... is a very imperfect test of responsibility' (1856: 22).

But who were these men who dared to rebuke?

The Alienists

A loosely defined collection of medics who saw exculpation in the disordered mind. Without them, more people would surely have walked to the gallows.

Amidst derogatory claims that their subject lacked science, they faced stringent resistance to appearing in court. When they did, their views met with disparaging comment, while discordant diagnoses only weakened their calls.

Internal divisions threatened derailment – when adversary counsel employed them to fight on both sides:

'Seeing that … it is known that experts … can be retained on both sides …, in the criminal courts all such evidence is viewed with such suspicion that I have known it to be the wisest course not to call for any medical opinion at all' (Rev. Lord Osborn in Smith 1981a: 120).

While their greatest enemy by far were the prominent judges, who dissuaded the juries from paying much heed:

'[A] jury should only receive evidence by which *ordinary* men can arrive at the fact of the state of mind'. Adding: '[B]etween these learned doctors, who is to determine?' (in Smith 1981a: 106, my *emphasis*).

The fatal verdicts it led to brought alienist howling, such that:

'We, in our turn, might make merry did it not happen that the difference of opinion among chief-justices, sometimes involves the hanging of a man, and, therefore, is no joking matter' (*JPM* 5: 104).

A change in their fortunes arrived via a respectable few – such as Professor Taylor (who grasped law as efficiently as madness), Bucknill, Maudsley, Winslow and more – each giving life to the incipient cause.

Criminal Responsibility

To some, the insane escaped the rigours of justice; to others, that mad men were unfairly hanged.

Isaac Ray, the father of American medical jurisprudence, tried his own definition for determining guilt:

'Was the accused insane at the time [of the act]? If so, has it nevertheless been proved ... that [the] crime was unrelated to [the accused's] mental disorder?' (in Walker 1968: 109).

His wording was clever – for the first time, the onus of proof moved from defence to the Crown. Where, traditionally, this had rested with the often bewildered defendant (later, his/her counsel), others thought *sanity* should be proved by *the law*. The confusion soon led to a glut of inconsistent decisions (*eg see* Davies or Pritchard and Turton – *Part 5*); while the outcome remained a matter of luck:

'[T]he great defect in English law is ... the uncertainty of its application.' Adding: '[A]n acquittal on the plea of insanity is ... a mere matter of accident' (Taylor in Bucknill 1857: [94]).

Crime and Punishment

On the one side, the mad still deserved to be punished; on the other that madness exculpated their crime? Assuming their involvement remained reasonably certain, should they be punished as criminals or treated as ill? As ever, it only led to confusion: that saw the sane man escape and the lunatic hanged.

Figures like Mayo (*see Part* 1) maintained the insane needed shaping, and should be used to deter those attracted to crime:

'I am far from affirming that all these unhappy persons deserved death; I only mean to suggest, that for the sake of preventive example, they required some form of punishment' (1847: 175).

While to others, the insanity plea was an easy way out. 'Shamming' was hard for the public to swallow, though Bucknill exploded the popular myths:

'When the jury has actually acquitted the prisoner on the ground of insanity, the judge has no power to send him to a lunatic asylum. He can only order the prisoner to be detained during the Queen's pleasure ... [until and only] ... the Secretary of State orders his removal ... *[on the strength of] certificates* of the prisoner's insanity, *signed by two medical men.*' (1856: 392, my *emphasis*).

He added with regret:

> 'Of this security against the evasion of justice, on the plea of insanity, the public are generally ignorant' (*ibid*).

Capital Punishment

The debates gained their rhythm in the face of a capital sentence; without death, their argument might have faded away. Individuals like Dymond, and groups (such as his Society for the Abolition of Capital Punishment), indirectly joined forces with the alienist camp.

Not always agreeing on the insanity *condition*, to have the sentence commuted was focus enough. Though it too only led to greater confusion, with often farcical verdicts from the insanity plea. Too often the law – in particular, the judges – placed more faith in lay juries than the alienist's view.

The inevitable outcome perhaps were post-trial 'corrections'.

Home Secretary's Trap

In the light of such uncertain conclusions, the means of 'correction' became the Home Secretary's curse (*eg see* Gallop, Hatto *et al Part 5*). With a power only afforded since Victoria's accession, his post-trial decisions were met with derision or glee. When he commuted the sentence of death to transportation or prison, it seldom appeased and more often annoyed.

His position was no more improved by another change in the statutes. Judges, who wished to avoid the fatal decision, simply *recorded* the sentence and left it for him to pronounce (*see Appendix 1*).

In numerous ways, it was the start of the end for capital verdicts – and threatened the future of the alienist pleas. With no threat to life for those now found guilty, juries were no longer inclined to hear the insanity plea.

A Statutory 'Answer'

(Unsatisfactory?) solutions came in confused Acts of Parliament, designed to resolve the crime and insanity debates. In 1800, Hadfield's 'acquittal' brought new swift legislation: the Criminal Lunatics Act now detained the insane until

His Majesty's Pleasure be known. The Insane Prisoners Act (1840) extended the same to those yet to stand trial. While two further Acts (1845) provided the requisite means: county asylums and overseers in law.*

And so ...

From Hadfield to M'Naghten and for years to come, men, women *and* children (eg *Allnutt – see Part 5*) endured the confusion from the heated debates. For more than a century – *and possibly still* – the mad faced a lottery: be pardoned or hanged.

---

* *See Appendix 1* for summarised statutes; *Part 1* for Lunacy Commissioners.

Chapter 4

Mad Women, Bad Women

A woman's particular place in the insanity debates rose typically from two disparaging slants: their connection to infanticide (murdering their children), and the ongoing appraisal in the masculine mind. Certain conditions *were* peculiar to women, at least as defined in a misogynist's world. Her nature, they said, was creative yet fickle: 'moister, looser' (Scull 2011: 14), and prone to decay.

'Monthly Madness'

Underpinning the view that women were trouble, the chauvinist world made much of the moon. Leastways, how it brought regular 'chaos'; her 'time of the month', every twenty-eight days…

In short, the 'strain' made women liable to madness and, by extension, a danger on account of their minds. Such prescribed conditions bore evocative titles – obstructed/suppressed menstruation, amenorrhea, *catamenial madness* – all of which meant she could be quite deranged.

When joined by that epitome of hormonal imbalance – the art of bringing life to the earth – attempts to control were excessive in number; and all could be found in both medicine and law:

'Women gave life, but at the cost of menstruation, emotional dependency, nervous weakness and a world view restricted to the family' (Smith 1981a: 144).

In these terms, *hysteria*, *neurasthenia*, and *uterine madness* became simply too hard for the men to ignore.

Predisposition I – Insanity

The nineteenth century view of women, madness and crime embraced four offensive assumptions:

1. A woman was corrupt, at least once a month
2. The role of women was explicit, in the natural order of things (ie she was maternal and gentle)
3. Those who were not, displayed *unnatural* madness
4. In both medicine and law, there must be a response.

Taylor, eminent forensics professor, proclaimed there was an undeniable connection:

> 'Disordered menstruation, owing to sympathy of the brain with the uterus, may ... operate as a cause ... of intellectual disturbance' (1873: 567).

Followed by warnings such things led to crime:

> 'At or about the time of puberty, especially if any cause of obstruction exist, females become irritable, easily excited, and they have been known to perpetrate, without motive, crimes of great enormity, such as murder and arson. A propensity to steal is also stated sometimes to manifest itself' (*ibid*: 300–01).

While, in particular, he highlighted the onset of menstruation:

> 'The case of Brixey (*see Part 5*), tried for the murder of an infant ... will serve as an illustration of the morbid effect produced on the brain by disordered menstruation ... [T]he state of the mind should be therefore carefully watched at this period of life, and any causes of violent excitement removed. Irregularity, difficulty, or suppression of the menstrual secretion may give rise to temporary insanity, indicated by taciturnity, melancholia, capricious temper, and other symptoms. Puberty in the male may be attended with similar morbid propensities, but these are not so commonly witnessed as in the female sex' (1873: 301).

John Burton, a *non-alienist* doctor – and witness in the same 1845 trial – expounded his own not-so-humble opinion:

'I … have frequently had occasion to attend young women who have been subject to temporary suspensions of the action of nature, and I believe any suspension of that action is calculated very much to derange the general constitution' (*The Times*, 17 February 1845).

Adding, with no little relevance:

'Sometimes the effect assumes an appearance as though the patient was labouring under dropsy, and occasionally, instead of affecting the body, it affects the head … dull chronic pains in the head and the region of the brain. This is attended with restlessness of manner, moroseness, and dullness of appearance. The patient is subjected also to fits of irritability and great excitement and passion' (*ibid*).

[Note the change in reference, from prisoner to patient.]

Not all doctors agreed. Suppressed menstruation, argued Combe at the start of the century, seldom caused madness as others defined:

'[I]n a great majority of the instances recorded as examples of this kind, the above phenomena were in reality the consequences, and not the causes, of the cerebral and mental affections' (1831: 147).

Thus, in crime, a woman's guilt could not be blamed on her irregular cycle, nor forgiveness expected when enduring the same.

The most perilous time, however, came not during menstruation, but in the period following a difficult birth. **Puerperal Insanity** (*see Part 2*) increased the chances of murder – as the mother rejected the new-born in violent terms.

In Victorian Britain, it became a principal focus, seen as the most dangerous madness on both sides of the line. It was, indeed, a rare mental condition – one where medicine and law had found common ground:

'Verdicts were extremely variable. Only with certain types of defendants – extremely deluded lunatics and infanticidal women – was there an *overlapping of medical and legal descriptions*' (Smith 1981a: 162, my *emphasis*).

Predisposition II – Crime

Cases blamed on menstrual disruption were never too hard for the alienists to find. Ann Shepherd (1845 – eg *ibid*: 156), for example who **stole** an expensive feather boa thanked 'suppression of the menses' for her acquittal in court. While Martha Brixey (*see above*), charged with killing an infant [not her own], used 'menstrual disturbance' as her insanity plea.

As **infanticide** became the scourge of nineteenth century Britain, this harrowing act brought the worst conundrum of all. Were these mothers who killed 'mad women' or 'bad women', destined to nurture yet killing their own?

Infanticide was a crime that:

'was formally murder, and needed deterrence as murder, but which [many] agreed should not actually be treated like murder' (*ibid*: 146).

As the body count rose, so did the excuses – and with them, an outcry to eclipse all the rest.

[For lengthy discussions, see Smith 1981a, Showalter 1987, Walkowitz 1994 and others].

Undue Compassion?

Case after case saw women acquitted – not on questions of guilt but on presumptions of 'why'. Why had she stolen? Why had she murdered? Both sides of the courtroom agreed on one thing: being a woman, she needed compassion.

As well as insanity, 'excuses' rained down: abandonment, want, women's submissive position … all reasons to pardon, not just from their minds.

In came a raft of unacceptable measures: penal servitude for life, transportation, and worse. Undeniably harsh, and with their own dire repercussions, but at least mothers who murdered escaped being hanged:

'There is no crime that meets with so much sympathy,' wrote Ryan, adding: '…often of the most ill-judged kind' (in Smith 1981a: 145).

Rebecca Smith, the last woman to swing for killing her child, was despatched to the gallows in 1849. Convicted of poisoning her child, she appeared to pay the price not so much for the murder, but because her weapon was arsenic, which suggested intent. [There were rumours she had done it before – a number of times.]

Many women saw mercy not from the jury, but after a trial and from one particular source: the Home Secretary, faced not just with claims of exculpatory madness, but a wider distaste for hanging 'their kind'. Post-trial commutations invariably led to stays in a county asylum [or Bethlem, Broadmoor or Fisherton House]; but many perceived it as an easy way out.

As more women were seen to be 'getting off free', the public and press started to wail. Headlines like 'she was not hanged because she was *pretty*' (eg *Weekly Dispatch* 18 May 1856) emblazoned the 'red tops' and ballads alike (see bibliography).

When the murdered child had been born out of wedlock – itself revealing illegitimate sex – the popular objections to undue compassion reached a crescendo like never before. Such *depravity* (*see Part 2*) meant women were escaping with murder, committed, some say, to bury their sins.

In a particular case (*see Part 5*), one woman's avoidance of a capital sentence was blamed for another [Martha Brown] being despatched to her death:

'Her execution was to set right what [the other's] reprieve had deranged. Error on the one side was to be counterpoised by error on the other' (*Caledonian Mercury* September 1856).

'The Female Malady'

Professor Showalter's term for the 'madness' of women highlighted social conditions of the Victorian age. As well as puerperal insanity, other 'gender conditions' denounced women as fragile, in need of repair. In the goldfish-bowl of women's 'conditions', alienists like Laycock (1840) and Prichard (1822) highlighted their role:

Hysteria was traditionally described as 'an attack of the vapours' – after the energies that supposedly rose from the troublesome womb. Its symptoms included erratic behaviour, complex yet abnormal movements, deformed positions and an uncontrolled thrashing of limbs. Even the production of 'urine' from the mouth – *hysterical ischuria* – became quickly regarded as par for the course.

Key to Thomas Laycock's hysteria theories was the exculpatory nature of its effect on the will (*see also Part 2*). By 'extending' the nervous system upwards, that is to take in the brain [where the spine entered the encephalon (contents of the skull)], he argued its damage brought uncontrollable acts. Such moments of 'reflex' behaviour became a cornerstone of *impulsive* or *volitional* madness that often appeared through the insanity plea.

[His cause was not helped when certain female defendants were accused of 'putting on' the condition in hope of reprieve. One, Jane Parnell, features in the collection of cases (*Part 5*).]

Neurasthenia – literally, a weakness of nerves, though by no means exclusive to women. In the era of great enterprise and industrialisation, nervous exhaustion and breakdown were common complaints. Rest cures for women – championed by Silas Weir Mitchell [and maligned ever since] – became a popular treatment. Mesmerism too attracted support, though it was quickly dismissed as little more than a hoax.

Though Laycock's *A Treatise on the Nervous Diseases of Women* (1840) may be read today as a misogynist's work, the impact of his views on neurasthenia might have helped them escape even the sentence of death:

> 'By extension, his belief in the nervous system as a responsible 'agent' could, he concluded, be of use in justifying a plea of insanity – because when the defendant is shown to have acted **impulsively** and/or without any **volition** [eg from neurasthenia], *then they must be considered insane*'
> (taken from criminalunacy.blogspot.co.uk, my *emphasis*).

Dealing in Pain

Such was the fear of wayward (if not always criminal) women, that unspeakable 'remedies' formed a cruel response. To be fair, most alienists and medical practitioners found them much too abhorrent, leading to those who practised being 'struck off'. The most infamous is included here for his part in the story.

Isaac Baker Brown, a name to provoke horror and outrage, pioneered the clitoridectomy as a means of control. This most controversial of all interventions, on the grounds of 'treating' so-called insanity ['diagnosed' by nymphomania, hysteria and sexual expression], it was dismissed as 'questionable, compromising, un-publishable mutilation' (quoted in Darby 2003).

He sought to justify the procedure by claiming that onanism (masturbation) caused all kinds of complaint – hysteria (again), epilepsy, mania, insanity – and eventually death!

Not content with mutilating the clitoris, Baker Brown turned his attention to the labia too. 'Endorsing' the procedure, he offered 'proof' of its value by relating the case of a victim who, post-operation, became a born-again Christian and 'obedient wife' (Showalter 1987: 76–77).

Conclusion

Though Victorian women suffered at the hands of their male oppressors, the attention they gained was a double-edged sword. Undoubtedly victims of misogynist bias – even outright perversion – they benefitted too from a desire to excuse.

Chapter 5

Case Histories

William Newton Allnutt – *'A very great danger to society'*

Wednesday 27 October 1847 – Poisoned his Grandfather; Irresistible Impulse, Hackney

The case of a *12-year-old boy*, William Allnutt, condensed many of the issues in the Victorian debates. From those connected with his supposed condition, to the appearance of medical witnesses in court; from an insanity plea to an intractable judge; from the verdict it garnered to its long-lasting effects. Together, they sum up neatly – and disturbingly – the tone of this book.

Samuel Nelme died on 27 October 1847, following a short but excruciating illness. And which, but for a post-mortem, would have passed unannounced. Following a series of tests, by a number of doctors,* old Nelme was discovered to have been unlawfully killed. To be exact, by consuming 'powered lump sugar', which his grandson, William Allnutt, had laced with a 'drug'.

Over a period of time, the boy had been adding arsenic in varying doses, but so little of it was eaten that it took longer than hoped. The fatal amount came from ironic misfortune, when Nelme sweetened the gruel he was taking to make himself well!

Medical History

So complicated was the case that the Old Bailey trial did not get under way until the end of the year. Once it did, there was immediate chaos – as Ballantine, the lad's barrister, lodged the insanity plea.

The circumstances behind William's apparent insanity were shown to be both accidental and fated. A nasty fall on a ploughshare when he was only

---

* Notably Dr Letheby, physician and lecturer on chemistry at the London Hospital – for his full account into the study of arsenic, *see Appendix 4.*

18 months old, not only severed his nose but broke a bone in his skull. [One medical witness now suggested it played 'mischief' with his under-formed brain.] And a subsequent slip on the ice had rendered him stupid – with an '[idiotic] expression' his mother proclaimed.

Some little time later, he began complaining of headaches and ever since then, his health had been poor … as he suffered with ring-worm [*scrofula*] which medical opinion defined as 'a disease of the head', though some disagreed [see McMurdo, below]. Somnambulism too, and terrifying nightmares, were both attributed to his unhealthy brain.

Yet it was his *hereditary* illness that attracted attention, with four family members being recorded insane. His father had suffered epilepsy in his final two years, leading to violence and drink by the time of his death. And two aunts each succumbed to *anmarosis* – 'a nervous disease' – no doubt arising from 'a disease of the brain'.

William's own particular 'insanity symptoms' were revealed to the court as he stood in the dock, including a desire for cruelty, provoked by the 'voices', which he consistently claimed he heard in his head:

'Do it, do it, you will not be found out' (*Old Bailey Proceedings Online*).

Expert Medical Witness

The jury now heard evidence from no less than *eight* separate medics – all but one had deduced he was likely insane. To most he had shown, by his eccentric behaviour, a certainty that one day in the future he would be utterly mad.

Edward Payne, the Allnutt's regular doctor, had previously warned of his young state of mind:

Court: 'Had it occurred to you to think him insane?'

Dr Payne: 'Yes; and I have expressed it before—I cannot say I thought him insane before October [when the murder occurred]; but I thought him eccentric and excitable.'

(Transcribed from *Old Bailey Proceedings Online*)

Edward Croucher, surgeon at Berkshire County Prison, believed the ploughshare incident had caused irreparable damage. Epilepsy and derangement would occur at some point in his life.

Dr Frederick Duesbury, who had treated William for scrofula less than twelve months before, revealed conversations with the boy, who he found to be peculiar and eccentric; concluding that he lacked 'a sound state of mind'. Crucially, he added that madness had not affected his power of reason [ie he knew right from wrong], but his *moral judgement* was already harmed. In short, he would have known administering poison would yet land him in trouble, but not that it was in any way morally wrong.

Dr Letheby, though no insanity expert, was next on the stand and 'confirmed' several things:

a)   'a disordered state of the brain' could be blamed for the boy's sleep-walking habits;
b)   hearing voices may likewise reveal the same;
c)   the injury he suffered in the fall on the ploughshare might 'give rise to an alteration in its [the brain's] formation';
d)   and the scrofula he suffered 'disorder[ed] the brain' (*Old Bailey Proceedings Online*).

The last expert witness, Dr John Conolly (*see Part 1*), had emerged as a leader in lunacy care. Superintendent of Hanwell Lunatic Asylum, he assessed young William while still on remand. He found the boy inherently troubled, 'that he [was] imperfectly organised…', and concurred with the others that his mind was 'unsound'. Then he added: 'I should think him very likely to become [wholly] insane' (*ibid*). He cited sleep-walking, night-terrors, scrofula, *and* his father's own madness, as proof his 'opinions' had basis in 'fact'.

The sole dissenter was Gilbert McMurdo, medical officer at Newgate, where William was held. Resisting claims he was ignorant on the subject of lunacy, he stood by his judgement the boy was 'correct'. There is 'a great distinction,' he continued, '…between what is called a disease of the mind and moral insanity'; and rejected suggestions that scrofula affected the brain. 'My opinion,' he concluded, 'is that the prisoner shows no indications of insanity whatever' (*ibid*).

Matters came to a head when William Ballantine, the boy's counsel, cross-examined McMurdo, the prison MO:

Ballantine: 'Am I right in supposing that almost in every case of insanity the moral faculties are the first to be implicated in the disorder? I am putting the question from Dr Winslow's book, which I conclude is one of high authority.'

McMurdo: 'I have read it, *it is not of very great authority* … I should consider that in an infant the mind is rather a matter of feeling than of understanding – they understand from others that a thing is right or wrong, and do not reason upon it….'

(ibid, my emphasis).

When later asked by the judge, Baron Rolfe: 'Did the boy appear to you to be a person capable of distinguishing between right and wrong?' McMurdo simply said: 'Yes'.

The Insanity Condition
Partial insanity was already a term being used to define William's condition. Payne believed it rendered him incapable of deducing right from wrong. He also considered the boy had acted on impulse, while suffering delusion – in his case, the voices that came in his head.

The notion of impulsive behaviour ('irresistible impulse') was supported by Duesbury. While Conolly, in thinking him certain to future insanity, believed it was more a derangement at this moment in time.

To the intractable baron, the diagnoses they gave in the end scarcely mattered – each flew in the face of the Rules and the law (*see Part 3* and *Appendix 3*). Besides, there was William's recent confession; a note to his mother explaining it all.

A Young Lad's Confession
Written ahead of his courtroom appearance, William confessed and expressed a fear for his life:

'My Dearest Mother … I have done what I am accused of. How I got the poison was this: on the 20 of Oct. grandfather went to his desk for the key of the wine-cellar to get some wine up and to look over his accounts; and whilst he was gone I took the poison out, and emptied some of it into another piece of paper, and put the other back; and then after dinner I put it in the sugar-basin; *and why I did it was I had made grandfather angry with something I had done, and he knocked me down into passage, and my head went up against the table and hurt it very much, and he said next time I did it, he would almost kill me*; but in future I will say the truth and nothing but the truth: as grandfather said, 'Truth may be blamed, but cannot be shamed.' *But if I am transported I know it will be the death of me*, therefore I hope they will pardon me. What is the punishment of man to the punishment of God? It is an awful thing to fall into the hands of the living God. I dare say you will not believe the dreams, but I assure you it is the truth. With kindest love to you and all at home, believe me, ever your affectionate son, W.N.A.' (*Old Bailey Proceedings Online*, my *emphasis*)

In Reaching a Verdict
Baron Rolfe vouchsafed his distaste for insanity as exculpation for murder. When he summed up the trial, he was typically firm (my *emphases*):

- they [the jury] were not duty-bound to accept the experts' opinions – 'if [they] did not accord with their own *common sense* and *experience*' of mind;
- they had the chance to put a check on frail-grounded defences – that 'might be attended with very disastrous results to society' if not to mankind;
- it was the *defendant's* responsibility to demonstrate madness [*see Davies etc, Part 5*] – and they should be satisfied there was proof he was not 'able to distinguish [a] *right from* [a] *wrong*';
- medical evidence had spoken of 'uncontrollable impulse' [his words], which the jury must treat with concern and alarm ['with such jealousy and suspicion, because it might tend to the perfect justification of every crime that was [ever] committed']!

(*The Times* 15 December 1847)

Their verdict perhaps revealed near-total confusion – probably matching the alienists' minds. William Allnutt was guilty of murder – but recommended mercy on account of his age. [In truth, they steered clear of an insanity verdict.]

Wary Compassion
Rolfe was jubilant yet understandably wary as he turned to his colleague for legal advice. At last, he accepted the jury's recommendation, but was typically earnest when expressing his mind.

Having 'rejoiced', he said, they had found the boy guilty of murder, he was equally happy that they ignored the insanity plea: a defence 'made in order to induce [them] to swerve from the strict path of duty ... [one] very frequently made, and ... too often [upheld]'.

He went on; further 'rejoicing' that 'the jury had thrown to the winds the idle sophistry by which the defence was to be made out on the present occasion' – that is, the unwelcome insanity plea. As he acknowledged their recommendation for mercy, he concluded that it was due to the defendant's tender years and 'not from any belief [he] was not in a sound state of mind', before adding: 'which was one in cases of murder, that, except in the present instance, he had never felt himself justified in paying any attention'!

(*The Times* 15 December 1847)

He *recorded* the death sentence – a legal 'opt-out' allowing commutation by the Home Secretary's hand (*see 'Home Secretary's Mercy'* – *Glossary*). One which, in time, saw him transported for life.

Final chapter

William Allnutt's fear that being transported *will be the death of me* came horribly true. Held for four years until he was 16 (the minimum age for transportation), he was kept first at Newgate Gaol then at Millbank before being shipped. At last, on 16 July 1851, he joined the convict vessel *Minden* and, within days, was admitted to its hospital suffering chronic *catarrh*. Arriving in Freemantle, Western Australia, he fell ill again within a paltry three months. This time his health was never to recover and he died of *phthisis*,* at just 17 years old.

---

* a wasting disease similar to consumption.

Joseph Baines – *'The nasty black cloud'*

Tuesday 6 June 1854 – Murder; Moral Insanity, Crowland, Lincoln

The singular and vicious case of Joseph Baines lit the fires of protest against the insanity plea. In particular, that most 'sordid of maladies', *moral insanity* (*see Part 2*), rejected by most. Thomas Mayo (*see Part 1*) objected to what he considered the insidious 'diagnosis', excusing guilty offenders deserving the rope. And when the press bemoaned Baines and his 'undeserved' let-off, they were left incandescent by what happened next.

On 6 June 1854, in the city suburb of Crowland in Lincoln, Joseph Baines, 38, was seen by a neighbour entering a house. Nothing unusual in that, for she knew Sarah Hickling, his 'mother',* was busy inside and was no doubt expecting her surrogate 'son'.

Minutes later, an awful truth was revealed. The woman came rushing outside in a terrible state. 'Murder! Murder!' She appeared to be fleeing. 'Murder!' she cried, before taking a fall.

In a flash, Baines was on her, a poker held skyward, a look in his eyes described later as 'wild'. Swinging the devilish weapon down on her body, he pummelled her head again and again. Now using both hands to grasp it much better, he continued the beating until he was sure she was dead.

Alerted by the commotion, frightened neighbours came running, but were sufficiently scared to keep a safe distance away. Baines threw down the iron and set off in a hurry, last seen absconding to the centre of town.

Faced with a murder, the people were hurried, and someone was sent to fetch the local police. But before they arrived, Baines returned to the murder, gathered the poker and set off again. Before he left, he took another swipe at her head!

This time, Ringrose, a shoemaker, had the foresight to follow, soon joined by the first constable to arrive at the scene. Ringrose named the pub that Baines had run into, and pointed him out before going within.

As the policeman approached, Baines lifted his head: 'You're looking very ill. Can you sleep at night?'

---

* In truth, the second wife of his father-in-law.

The constable – who, it has to be said, *had* been suffering greatly – ignored the question, but Baines offered more: 'I cannot [sleep]. The other night, I got up and ran to Peterborough [some fifty miles southward].'

He then put his hands to his face and cried out in pain: 'Oh! My head! Oh! My poor wife! Oh! My poor children!' all the while sobbing and stamping the floor. Then, without warning, he ended his wailing, his sorrow forgotten, as composed as before: 'Never mind, a good run or walk will soon see me right!'

Lincoln Castle

On 25 July, Baines was put on trial at the Lincoln Assizes, held in the castle at the top of the hill. The courtroom was told he had suffered a trauma that changed his behaviour in just a few months. Gone was the dutiful husband and peace-loving father, displaced by a monster; morose and depressed.

As the trial continued, they heard of his inexplicable worry – in particular his fortunes, though he was well placed. Yet still his fear was real and an example was cited, accepted by some as undeniable proof:

A man 'superior in station' had come to Lincoln to order a suit. Baines, being a tailor, and a good one at that, was called on and invited to tender, but for some inexplicable reason ignored the request. It was later cited as the start of his fall, as both trade and his health suffered a steady decline. Described now as vacant and sullen, observers had worried he was losing his mind.

At this point in the trial, several medical witnesses were ordered to give their opinion to support such a claim. Frequently cited was *hereditary madness*, as a family insanity was laid before court. Both his sisters and mother were apparently troubled, while the asylum physician was sure of one thing. With such a strong set of factors, not least from his mother, he was likely insane at the time of his crime.

Asked then about the condition he suffered, they suggested Prichard's *moral insanity* – or 'homicidal orgasm' as it was derogatorily known (*see Part 1*).

The press and the public sensed a miscarriage of justice: the trial was preparing to save the man from the rope. Presiding judge, Justice Maule, incurred the wrath of critics like Mayo, who thought both he and his jury were being easily led. One erstwhile volume likened their kind to an '*imbecile* jury' (*Fraser's Magazine* 51: 257) – after all, turning down work was no reason to kill!

When Baines was declared not guilty, on the ground of insanity, not even Her Majesty's Pleasure (*see Glossary*) would silence the storm. He arrived at

Bethlem Hospital, the then State Criminal Lunatic Asylum, on 11 October 1854. He was a man said to harbour the luck of the Devil, and was hated for acting with Satan in mind.

Moral Insanity

As fate decreed, Baines had committed his murder, just *four days* before Brough (*see Part 5*) pushed his case from the news.

To certain observers, he would not be so favoured, as both cases were cited for alienist abuse. A year after the trial – reporting on Mayo's earlier *Croonian Lecture* – *Fraser's Magazine* tore holes in the insanity plea. His defence was founded on a risible condition [*moral insanity*] – was not every crime the result of moral decay?

A caustic assault drove home their disgust:

> 'To use the language of an experienced official commenting on the Esher [Brough] case, "[t]he nasty black cloud is no new dodge!"' (*Fraser's Magazine* 51: 255).

Repeating their attack against Baines' acquittal, they poured scorn on Prichard and his 'laughable' work:

> '[Dr Mayo] has shown that [where] the plea of "moral insanity" was set up as an excuse for crime, deserved no better appellation than that of "brutal recklessness", and that to acquit criminals of this class on the ground of irresponsibility, is only to induce others to follow in the same course, who might otherwise be restrained by a wholesome fear of punishment' (*ibid*: 247).

Like the rest of the press, they rejected the asylum, as a comfortable sidestep to the sentence of death!

Much Better – Far Worse

Their unbridled anger can well be imagined when, less than eight years later, Baines received a further reprieve. On 18 September 1862, he was declared fully recovered: the lunatic killer no longer a threat.

At this point, he might well have reflected how lucky he was … Had he been found 'Insane on Arraignment' (*eg see Turton – Part 5*), he could now be recalled as 'fit to stand trial'. But having been acquitted insane (at the moment he murdered), he was given his freedom … and allowed to go home.

His return was met with predictable fury, from those who had witnessed first-hand his attack. Entering the street, he met with a neighbourly 'welcome': with the windows 'put in' and a placard nailed to the door on which someone announced Baines as the 'Lincolnshire killer' – an epitaph he doubtless found hard to live down.

Edwin Bates – *Triple Jeopardy*

July 1850 – Attempting to extort money from HRH Prince Albert; 'Self-Proclaimed' Insanity, London

Edwin Bates, 38, had a troubled history with money ... especially when he tried to recover his loss. On at least three separate occasions over more than a decade, he faced time behind bars for breaching the peace. One feature throughout was his *self-proclaimed* madness – if only somebody had listened, no-one need have got hurt.

Bates' first offence, around the time of Victoria's accession, led to two months in prison. His second, weeks later, happened while still behind bars! His latest, in July 1850, saw him charged with extortion – from Prince Albert himself!

London, c. June 1837

Bates' woes centred on a railway investment which had, literally, come off the rails for him. Feeling aggrieved that his purchase of shares in the Northern & Eastern Railway Company (NERC) had plunged by significant value, he claimed he had been grossly misled by those on its Board.

In front of the magistrates, he confessed to having sent letters to Charles- to to Rowcroft, Company Secretary, in which he demanded his money – or he would end the man's life. Confined for two months in Mansion House prison, what should have been an end to the matter, within weeks, became worse.

While still behind bars, supposedly full of contrition, Bates wrote two further letters, both dated in June. Addressing them this time to Bagshaw, the company chairman, he repeated demands for the money he had lost.

Expecting compensation of £150, he peppered the missives with a number of threats. For Bates was consistent in 'resolving' his troubles – no money forthcoming meant someone must die. Unsurprisingly, Bagshaw brought criminal charges.

London Guildhall, September 1837

On 16 September 1837, Edwin Bates – now 25 and described as an artist of 'respectable appearance' – took to the stand in London's Guildhall. Charged with demanding money with menaces ... the authorities were wary of his ambition to kill.

Alderman Venables observed that, whatever Bates' rights to feeling disgruntled, the country could never condone an unlucky investor, who said 'I'll shoot you through the head if you don't pay me the money I have lost!' (*The Times* 18 September 1837).

Bates further sullied his chances when, at the time he was arrested, was found to be in possession of at least one loaded gun; and again, when he confessed that he would have shot Rowcroft, had he not been on bail and keeping the peace!

Bates was committed for trial at the Central Criminal Court.

Old Bailey, 18 September 1837

At the Old Bailey trial, he confirmed both letters were his. Lengthy extracts were read out to the incredulous court:

'You by your numbers, and by the law, evade the oportunity (*sic*) of defence which the more honourable thief offers. Would to God that you were all comprised in one mass, that I might have one chance, to punish by my single arm the villany (*sic*) of the whole party. As I would hope for forgiveness for shedding the blood of the thief who attacks my property and my life, so shall I hope for forgiveness in heaven if my fury falls on the head of one or more of you ...'

Blaming Rowcroft for much of his suffering, Bates continued in his irrational tone:

'Could any man, with a heart in his *brest* (*sic*) stand by, as you have done, to see me perish? Knaves and villains all! look at my first letter to the company; and what man amongst you will say I am not a murdered man?...Before I was utterly lost I wrote to you to do me justice; but, instead of which, through that liar, knave, and coward, Rowcroft, the filthy instrument through whom you do your dirty work, I was *no* only *robed* of my money (*sic*), but my very means of life were cut off by the treachery of that vile thing. I would have saved myself by honourable industry; but the means which were my own then, had you promptly said you would do nothing for me, were sacrificed by the delay, as well as knavery, of your foul servant. Instead of blood, a green and sulphurous matter fills his veins, which, when he goes to hell, will burn and stink, and make the damnedest hell fouler. My all is gone. I am now in debt. I have not yet received one shilling by my profession; and, as you may naturally suppose, I cannot paint nor dig; to beg I am ashamed. *Madness is inevitable.*'

He finally arrived at his point [the letters were *much* longer!], by conveying his feelings in sinister terms:

'I now demand 132*l* 9*s*, one hundred and thirty-two pounds nine shillings, or I will have blood, for my blood, which you would spill.'

(Transcribed from *Old Bailey Proceedings Online*)

Mr Ryland, Bates' counsel, was forced to admit: 'it would not be safe to allow [him] to go at large in his present state of excitement... [until] his unfortunate delusion had passed away.' Crucially adding: '[when] he was restored to his right reason...' (*The Times* 23 September 1837). It was as close to the insanity plea as Bates was ever to get.

To no avail. The jury found Bates guilty of threatening behaviour, and the judge, Justice Vaughan, gave him twelve months in gaol. Yet the plaintiff (John Bagshaw) demanded the court show some mercy! To which Vaughan gave him his wish – and respited the term.

INTERLUDE: Central Criminal Court, January 1849

As a bizarre interlude, Edwin Bates found himself back in the court, though this time the *victim* of a horrid attack (the following based on *Old Bailey Proceedings Online*):

On 16 January 1849, walking home across Hungerford Bridge, a woman, Mary Flood, approached him and asked for the time.

As he pulled his watch from his pocket, she pressed him tight to the wall and threw a punch to his head.

No sooner had he returned to his senses than a man, Edward Smart, stepped out of the shadows, at first brushing him down and then helping him up. Catching hold of his arm, Smart gestured to Mary. 'I think, Sir, you've been taking some liberties' of the improper kind!

Bates was astounded. And in the ensuing confusion ... found his watch had been swiped.

Back in court, and no doubt fearing proceedings – assuming his own claims of madness were actually true – he waited, befuddled and frightened, as the jury delivered its verdict: Smart and Flood were found guilty ... transported ten years.

Bow Street Police Court, July 1850

Bates was a man who always liked to bear grudges! Some thirteen years later, he found himself back on the stand. Far from resigning himself to his pecuniary losses, he bolstered his efforts by focussing high. Gone were his missives to the men of the railway: none less than Prince Albert himself would do now.

At the hearing, he claimed to have been visited by a gentleman caller, who spoke with His Highness' authority with an offer to make. The Prince, he alleged, wished to 'contribute a small sum' of money, to a fund he supported in lieu of Bates' plight.

Colonel Grey, the Prince's assistant, presented several letters – Bates proudly confirming each one was his own – and though their contents would remain forever a secret, both Grey and the magistrate agreed they caused harm.

Bates now denied that was ever his intention – and explained they were written from a weakening mind.

Bates' (self-proclaimed) Insanity Plea

Bates put forward his own plea of insanity, insisting others thought him quite mad, if not strange in the head:

> 'I hope your Worship will consider the state of my mind at the time of writing these letters, and put a favourable construction upon them ... I had no hostile design in writing to Prince Albert. Dr Monro, Dr Sutherland, and Sir Peter Laurie can speak as to the state of my mind' (*The Times* 25 July 1850).

Referencing his past indiscretions, he went on unabated:

> 'I was tried for felony at the Old Bailey, thirteen years ago, [when] I was considered insane. I do not wish to speak of my own weakness, but it is well known that I am not right in my mind' (*ibid*)

And concluded by blaming his railway misfortunes as the cause of his ills!

The magistrate, Mr Jardine, denied it was neither his nor the court's role to respond to his problems; theirs was, quite simply, to try on the charge. On that, he was found guilty of attempted extortion. Poor Bates was bound over for £500.

With no means to settle the fine, Edwin Bates was 'locked up' (*ibid*). Whether as a victim of theft, or his errors of judgement, Bates' problems with money, it seemed, had not gone away.

Postscript

In an age when the alienists were condemned for false certification (eg *see Pownall*), Bates' self-proclaimed lunacy attracted no help. Few comments, even those written long after, lucidly supported his insanity plea. But one thing remained: he was as troubled by money as he was by his mind.

Isabella Blyth – *Blyth's Spirits*

Tuesday 25 November 1851* – Murdered her mother; 'Deprived of her Reason', Balbirnie Burns, Markinch, Fife

Isabella Blyth, a woman of 50, felt decidedly ill. She had said so, repeatedly, on numerous occasions. Nor was she alone in her findings, others agreed with that 'fact'. The difference, however, was that whilst Isabella may have thought she was sick in her body, everyone else thought she was sick in her mind.

Uncertain Beginnings

From the outset, there was uncertainty about both the case and the victim; officials were unsure of the plainest of facts.

'Grace or Grizzel or Girzy Duncan or Blyth …' nonetheless was the accused's natural mother. The murder weapon too attracted such scope: 'a pair of tongs, or other instrument or instruments, to the prosecutor unknown …' While the date of the crime* was 'set' as '25 November 1851, or on one or other of the days of that month, or of October immediately preceding, or of December immediately following …' It offered no hope to the one in the dock …

An Unsettled Woman

Two years before, after working in service, Isabella Blyth returned to her childhood home. Her mother, now well in her eighties, threw her arms open – Balbirnie Burns would know her daughter again.

At first, all seemed to go well but, with time passing slowly, things started to change. For weeks, Isabella grew ill-humoured and restless; complaining of headaches and staying in bed.

When pressed on the topic, she spoke of pitiful feelings – and confessed she was worried there was something wrong in her head.

As weeks passed to months, and months into years, her mother related her growing unease. Isabella's condition – howsoever determined – had never been worse than it seemed to be now.

---

* Mary Blyth, Isabella's sister-in-law, and others, said in their testimony at court the date of the assault was 25 November.

An Unforeseen Crime

On 25 November, Mrs Wilson – the Blyths' neighbour – was alerted by the shrieks of her 6-year-old boy. Racing round to the cottage, and finding the door still propped open, she peered in the darkness and called out the old woman's name.

The house appeared empty, there was silence within. Had her son been mistaken by what he had seen? Then she heard it, the terrible banging – 'as though something metal was striking at coal'. And the groaning voice of the dear old woman, a piteous pleading that caused her alarm.

Wilson called out again, but there was no more forthcoming, aside from the banging which had now grown so loud.

Mrs Dalrymple, another petrified neighbour, came to her shoulder and squinted within. As she did, Isabella Blyth appeared from the small room to the rear, walked across to the fire and hung up the tongs. The place she had come from was old Grace's bedroom.

'What's the matter with mother?' Dalrymple asked Isabella.

Cold Isabella answered with little surprise. 'Nothing.'

Yet the groans were still coming. 'Should you not go and see what's the matter?' Mrs Wilson was worried.

Isabella turned her back. 'Gang yersell!' was all she replied.

Now came old Grace's voice, weak but determined. 'Oh! Come to me, come to me … for [I am] killed!'

Waiting no longer, Wilson entered the bedroom, and found the old woman stretched out on the floor.

'Oh [hen], whatever's the matter?' So much blood seeped from her head, the white flannel cap was the colour of wine. Dalrymple now joined them, alarmed by the chatter, and the two women helped Grace to a chair in the warm.

It was Wilson who spoke, in a terrified whisper: 'Grace – have you fallen – have you had a bad fall?'

'No –' She could barely speak for the horror. 'Bell… she has struck me. With the [fireside] tongs.'

Wilson turned on Isabella,: how could she have done such a hideous thing?

Isabella's voice though was cold, enough for Hell to freeze over. 'Did you see me?' she challenged – which of course no-one had.

A shocked Mrs Wilson watched as the woman departed, and implored old Dalrymple to go and get help.

'If she dies, it means murder!'

Dr Grace, the local medical surgeon, was a full day too late to help poor Grace Blyth. When he paid the first of a series of visits, his patient was already slipping away. Dalrymple and Wilson looked in at every occasion, making sure the poor woman was never alone with her girl.

By the 29 November – when Isabella was finally arrested – everyone feared her mother would die. When that happened at length, on 4 December; the imprisoned young woman faced a capital charge.

Come to Trial

By the time the case reached the Perth Circuit Court, more than sixteen weeks later, the officials had heard rumours that Isabella Blyth was insane. Dr Grace, though, the same who had 'failed' her mother, insisted the daughter was fit to stand trial.

On the 29 April 1852, the Bench then heard from the strangest of witness – the *dead woman's* statement was read out in court. It had, they confirmed, been taken as gospel, given by her 'as in the prospect of death':

> '[Isabella] is not very sound of mind; she was generally quiet, but was sometimes excited ... all of a sudden she took up the tongs, and struck me on the left side of the head two or three times. There was no quarrelling at the time, and I gave her no cause for striking me' (Shaw 1853: 572–73).

How those revelations must have broken her heart.

Several witnesses were asked if they knew any better. All but one thought Bella was as sane as the rest. Mrs Wilson, for one, said 'she saw no symptoms of insanity about her' (*ibid*: 569); while Mrs Dalrymple was quick to retort: 'I never heard it said by neighbours that she was wrong in her mind' (*ibid*: 570).

One voice stood apart from the general agreement: Her sister-in-law, Mary, who felt sure she was mad. Indeed, she had thought so when she had twice asked Isabella why she assaulted her mother ...

> 'the first time she replied: "it was a pity she [was] not dead" – that "she should have been dead [a] long [time] ago!";

> the second time simply: "[I do] not know"' (*ibid*:571).

When asked why she had formed her fatal opinion, Mary made observations that removed any doubt: 'She always complained of a pain in her head,' she told them in earnest; which had worsened, it seemed, from the day she came home. She complained too of a 'roaring noise in her head ... like thunder'; and she gave the impression she thought Mary could hear it as well (*ibid*: 572).

The witness continued.: her words changed the mood of the ongoing trial ... It was not just her head; she believed her face and her back were in danger of wasting, and her nose ... oh, her nose, that was what bothered her most. "There is a discharge coming from it," she sobbed, when confronted by Mary; and, as though it confirmed it: "I can't bear the smell." With no sense she was lying, she continued her pleading: "It is falling off my face, by degrees, and will soon be off altogether." Though Mary confirmed she had seen nothing wrong (*ibid*).

Mary concluded by reporting a look of wild excitement, on many occasions, though not all the time. She reported how Isabella had changed, from being always so tidy, to one with little respect for herself or her things. She was, she reported, always wringing her hands, twisting the bed sheets as though tormented by thoughts.

Family Dilemma

Before Mary stood down, she made one more fearful confession. That the family had considered putting Isabella away. Her manner had worsened enough to inquire at the local asylum, but they had decided on caution to avoid making a scene.

When asked who had been consulted as part of the process, she pointed to a man at the back of the court. Dr Baillie, local surgeon, was called as a witness – and his testimony confirmed what the others now thought.

He believed Isabella suffered more than straightforward hypochondria – she was convinced her nose, and her hands, were wasting away. No matter how hard he tried, he could not reassure her; either through medical opinion or rank common sense.

He too had noted her vacant expression, how her symptoms had worsened in the previous six months. She was ill in her mind, if not in her body; certainly nothing that kept her confined to her bed.

He added, no doubt aware of the law since M'Naghten's trial (*see Part 3*): 'Sometimes she did, and sometimes she did not, *know right from wrong...*'

On her actual condition, his answer was simple: '[H]er spirits at times were very much depressed … [at other times] wild and unsettled'. Both he and her family agreed she was going insane.

Direct To A Verdict

Though other witnesses had yet to appear – among them, Dr Grace, who *still* vouched Isabella was sane enough to stand trial – Lord Cockburn,* Lord Chief Justice, interrupted the court. He confirmed, in his considered opinion, her plea of insanity had been sufficiently proved. If the jury agreed, he announced, they could arrive at their verdict; they did, and they said so in clinical terms:

> '… the pannel [defendant in Scotland] killed her mother in the way and manner mentioned in the indictment; but find it proven, that at the time the pannel was insane, and deprived of her reason' (Shaw 1853: 574).

Lord Cockburn now turned to poor Isabella, and declared she was no longer a subject of crime. The court 'assoilzied her simpliciter' (*see Glossary*), there was no case to answer, as defendant on trial she was free to stand down.

However, using uncertain rights in his role as a justice, he ordered she be sent back to Cupar to the gaol whence she came. And to remain there:

> '*during all the days of her life*, or at least ay and until farther orders of the Court of Justiciary with regard to her' (Shaw 1853: 574).

As had happened often in England, she had been found insane, enough to keep her away from the rope. But in the absence of reason, she was sent back to gaol, and on paper at least held no hope of reprieve.

In fact, Isabella Blyth was transferred to Perth General Prison, where she was recorded insane yet offered no help. At some point, however, her case courted compassion – for she died *four decades* later as an inmate at the asylum for Fife and Kinross.

---

* Lord Cockburn's posthumous memoirs recorded how, when asked why she had murdered her mother, Blyth replied: 'Weel, had she no lived lang eneuch?' He reflected her insane condition in colourful language: '[Her] reason had been gradually leaving her for two years, till at last it was gone, and she passed her time in visionary misery in bed. One of her prevailing alarms was for her nose, which seemed a very respectable article; but she was convinced that it had got black, and was going to fall off.' He also revealed how she had been 'disappointed' when she discovered she was not to be hanged. (1889:381).

Martha Brixey – *The Notorious 'Nanny'*

Sunday 4 May 1845 – Murder; Homicidal Mania/Moral Insanity/ Irresistible Impulse, Greenwich

18-year-old Martha Brixey was, to all who knew her, a most likeable girl: nurse to the children of a respectable family, commended for her character and flair for her work. It rendered the hideous events of an otherwise ordinary day all the more shocking and hard to explain.

Trouble Brewing

After three years in service with John Finch, solicitor, and his wife, Georgiana, Brixey displayed some worrying traits. Where once she was happy and a diligent worker, her moods were now sinister, dark and morose.

The greatest concern was her impatience with children – especially the three she was employed to protect.

Early in spring, following a family bereavement, she tried on a mourning dress she had been ordered to wear. Though repeatedly altered, at her own unrelenting insistence, she loathed how it looked on her delicate frame. Ripping it from her shoulders, she tore the skirt from the bodice, and prodded the latter deep in the grate. She screeched, as the top was caught by the fire: 'I wish the dress to the Devil!' was all she would say.

For the staid Mrs Finch, it proved too much to stomach: one more episode like this and she would be shown the door. And when Martha returned, the dress remade with new fabric, her mistress was frantic – and true to her word. Martha Brixey was given notice to quit.

Joined later that evening by Sarah, a servant, Martha grew resolute in her sense of despair:

> 'I need not make myself so very unhappy as I do,' she admitted. '[O]ne would think … I had committed murder, but I [know I] have not!'

Her colleague was shocked: 'Martha, do not talk in that way! I hope you will never be guilty of … a crime [such] as that.'

Martha continued, un-swayed by the warning: 'Do you ever know if a woman [has] hanged?'

'Why, if they commit murder they are hanged as well as men!' the servant relented, uneasy now where the conversation might lead.

'Then I would as soon as be hung (*sic*),' replied Martha, with scant interruption, 'as transported or put in a madhouse [for the rest of my life]!'

4 May 1845

The following day, 4 May, though not her usual duty, Brixey nursed the youngest child in the family – Robert, eight months. Afterwards, she joined the housemaid in the kitchen below; though her chores were refusing to focus her mind. At length, she blurted out her burning frustration: 'Oh! Elizabeth, Elizabeth I wish I was dead!'

A short while later, she re-approached Sarah, the servant: 'Do you think Mrs Finch will allow me to stay?'

'I think not.' The other girl could only be honest. 'She is not to be moved.'

Martha stood biting her nail in silence. 'Then I shall *not* leave. For I am not letting someone else take my place.'

Pressure Building

At around ten in the morning, the housemaid followed Martha into the pantry, and watched as she took the table knife from its box on the shelf. 'What are you doing?'

Martha tested the blade with her finger and thumb. 'I wish to cut a pencil for Miss Mary [the Finches' daughter].'

'The small one would do better,' said Elizabeth, perhaps growing uneasy.

She put it with the other. 'I will take both.' Adding: 'It will do to cut the bread and butter for the children'.

Elizabeth watched as she disappeared upstairs.

Only a few moments later, a scream drowned the household in impromptu despair.

Martha, having already rushed down the stairs, burst into the room where the Finches and the magistrate, Traille, were taking their tea.

'Oh, Sir! What have I done?'

Finch leapt to his feet. 'What!'

'Will you forgive me! Oh, Sir, I am a murderer! Good God, I have cut the dear baby's throat!'

Pushing her aside, he raced for the stairs.

In the room at the rear of the nursery, his eyes fixed on a scene of slaughter and death.

Poor Robert's head was almost detached from his body! His throat had been cut with such force the blade had severed the spine. The large table knife had been laid on his torso. Both it and the child were covered in blood.

As Finch descended the stairs, Traille came up at a canter, having restrained Georgiana from reaching the scene. Seeing Martha, who had moved to his study, Finch raced to confront her but it was she who spoke first.

'Oh, Sir, will you forgive me? What have I done?' Then added: 'What will become of me now?'

She grabbed at his sleeve, but he tossed her aside. 'You wretch! You have murdered my child! You will be hanged! *That* is what will become of you!'

She fell to her knees. 'Do you think God will forgive me, if I ask pardon and repent?'

He turned on his heels and sent for the police.

Central Criminal Court

Brixey's trial occurred within two weeks of the killing. Like so many before (and many more since), she was helped to the dock and afforded a chair.

William Bodkin, prosecuting on behalf of the nation, wasted no time in suggesting her mad. Her guilt, he admitted, was beyond all reasonable question, but reminded the court that the onus was hers. He apprised them of the Rules (*see Appendix 3*), still just two years since their making, and why they *must* be applied in a case such as this:

> 'What is the law respecting alleged crimes committed by persons afflicted with insane delusions in respect of one or more particular subjects or persons? As, for instance, when at the time … of the crime, the accused knew he (*sic*) was acting contrary to law' (*The Times*, 17 May 1845).

The answer given at the time by the group of eminent judges was, in Bodkin's opinion, remarkably clear:

> 'Assuming that your Lordship's inquiries are confined to those persons who labour under such partial delusions … and are not in other respects insane, [the prisoner] is punishable according to the nature of the crime

committed, if [they] knew at the time … [they acted] contrary to … law' (*ibid*).

This, he concluded, was the opinion of lawyers, not some irresolute alienists the jury were destined to hear.

An Insanity Case – made by Clarkson, defence counsel
Everything began with a report from Burton, the Finch family doctor, who had attended on Brixey a short time before. In the months leading up to the murder, he confirmed, she had suffered 'blocked menstruation', an exculpatory condition that affected her mind. Further, he added, it had rendered her sombre; with morbid obsessions that left her dull and morose. What's more, just three days before the diabolical murder, she complained of a headache she found hard to ignore.

When questioned by counsel, he confirmed he had advised Mrs Finch to send Brixey away:

'She had exhibited violence of temper, in tearing and burning her dress—I thought such an act of violence unfitted her to be among young children' (*ibid*).

When pressed again, he disclosed some startling impressions:

'I have known instances where the functions of the mind of a woman so situated [ie suffering obstructed menstruation] have been seriously affected'.

Though he would not be drawn on whether he thought Brixey insane.

'That is a very difficult question to answer.'

It was an unhelpful reply.

(above based on *Old Bailey Proceedings Online* unless otherwise stated)

Next, Sergeant Booth, of the Greenwich division, recounted her conversation as they walked through the station-house garden after her arrest: 'She asked me if I thought she would be hung or sent across the water in chains? Would Mr Finch forgive her in a week's time? [And] … whether she would have to wear a prison dress in Newgate, or be allowed to wear her own?'

During the course of the hearing, defence medical experts expressed their opinions, in what they considered a trying and most difficult case. There was no doubting her guilt, she had admitted the murder; and possessed awareness that she had committed some wrong. Nonetheless – the Rules and 'right-wrong test' notwithstanding – poor Martha Brixey was surely insane.

Clarkson had planted doubts about Brixey; but he needed something more concrete to get the jury onside. He now stepped up and addressed them directly; it was they who would save her or allow her to hang.

It was pointless, he argued, to examine the killing; his client had obviously slaughtered the boy! Nor did he question the Rules, at least not in their meaning – but he was certain each case should be judged on its own. He also hoped they would not be scared of compassion, nor fear the sort of reprisals an acquittal might bring [cf M'Naghten – *Part 3*]. Finally, he accepted Burton's first observations: that the accused was very 'likely insane'.

What he now outlined to a wavering jury were the critical signs of her mental decay: her crime lacked a motive [subsequently called into question]; it was all out of character [some voices opposed]; and her unusual 'wildness' [all accepted she had once been so peaceful] were symptoms of someone completely deranged.

He had, in effect – though he may well not have known it – argued for an *irresistible impulse* to murder; something, others believed, was the first case of its kind.

Summing Up and Decision
Presiding judge, Lord Chief Justice Denman – one of the fifteen whose answers led to the Rules – reminded the jury that only they could determine the outcome and that the verdict must reflect whether she had known a right from a wrong. But then he muddied the waters; by allowing a chance of survival – the Rules would not be applied if she suffered 'a deranged state of mind'.

The jury took just half an hour before the foreman delivered:

'That from the derangement of the system, which led to great excitement
in the prisoner at the time she committed the act, we are of the opinion
that she was not responsible for her actions' (*The Times*, 17 May 1845).

Denman's response, it seems, was full of compassion: 'That is, in fact, a verdict
of not guilty on the ground of insanity.' Then he looked to the clerk: 'Let it be
so' (*ibid*).

His last act was to order Martha Brixey should be detained, during Her
Majesty's Pleasure. The 18-year-old girl had avoided the rope.

Alienist Wisdom

Having revealed the verdict, we can now report medical reaction, expressed
after her trial had drawn to a close.

On what condition should the jury have accepted her defence of insanity?
Some pointed out she experienced no type of *delusion*, a pre-requisite for
madness in light of the Rules. Others conjectured she was used as a scapegoat,
alienists inventing an illness to further their cause.

In hindsight, numerous voices thought the plea had been destined to fail.
True madness, they said, was never shown to occur. Sir Alexander Morison,
visiting physician at Bethlem, lamented an absence of insanity that meant only
one thing. The plea relied not on the mind, or manner, of the guilty defendant,
but on the complexion of the hideous crime. This was, he exclaimed: '[A] species
of evidence…of a dubious nature' (1848: 456); and added Martha Brixey should
have been hanged. '[A]lthough many contend that it is better to let ninety-nine
criminals escape, than that one person of diseased mind should be sacrificed,
I cannot help thinking, that *severity in such extremely doubtful cases is the most
merciful error of the two in the end*' (*ibid*: 456–57).

Others saw her case as a medical breakthrough – the herald of *irresistible
impulse* (*see Part 2*) in the insanity plea. Inextricably linked with Prichard's
new *moral insanity* (*see Part 2*), Lockhart Robertson saw Brixey as a changer of
reason; the doubtful condition had no premise in law. When the jury acquitted,
they acted out of compassion. Or, as he preferred: 'the girl escaped hanging in
spite of the law' (1847: 171).

Many alienists, in fact, were left berating the verdict – decisions like these
were turning people away. If, as they feared, the 'insanity plea' was allowed to
run riot, others – more innocent – would soon have to pay.

Aftermath

Brixey's future, though, still hung in the balance. She might be alive, but under what terms? Not that the press or the public were inclined to forgiveness – and vented their spleens at her *lucky* escape.

At the start of 1846 (see Mayo 1847: 178), she was admitted to Bethlem, perhaps as Alexander Morison had already known. After meeting her twice, Thomas Mayo, moral insanity's fiercest critic, was only too happy to quickly denounce:

> 'The Greenwich Murderess … will afford very mischievous evidence to all
> such hysterical young females … how comfortably life may to appearance
> be spent after the indulgence of splenetic cruel, provided a human being
> is destroyed. There is not about her the smallest evidence of insanity'
> (1847: 174–75).

Living with Death

After arousing such heartless emotions, the story of Brixey disappeared from view. Just as well, for within thirteen years she was back out on the streets [cf *Baines – Part 5*]. Sadly for her, in the literal sense.

Though now at large, the poor woman had nothing to keep her. Over the next forty-five years [she lived beyond 74], she moved between the workhouse and lodgings, in a life of perpetual want. In 1873, her madness returned – spending thirteen long months in Colney Hatch lunatic asylum, from where she was later discharged, again considered 'improved'.

At all other times, she made use of the workhouse to an increasing degree. Registered 'not able-bodied', she grew increasingly desperate – though her experience of life had left her wiser than most. So that, at the turn of the century, she appears to have stayed at *two* neighbouring institutions, as she doubled her efforts to avoid starvation or worse. How often, in the recent half-century, must she have wished she had swung from the rope?

At last, Martha Brixey died a pauper in the summer of 1904. Unmarried and having brought no new life to the Earth to replenish the one she had taken, her eventual passing went largely ignored.

Mary Ann Brough – *Brough Justice*

*Saturday 10 June 1854 – Multiple Infanticide; Moral Insanity/Irresistible
Impulse, Esher, Surrey*

The tragic case of Mary Ann Brough, former wet-nurse to the future King
Edward VII, not only highlighted difficulties in judging someone wicked or mad
– it exposed the thorny issue of diagnosing conditions and an alienist movement
that was fighting itself.

Background

Mary Ann Brough was a tired, fretful, middle-aged woman. Married and
mother to seven young children, six of whom still resided at home. Latterly, she
was prone to dark moods and bouts of depression, accompanied by headaches
and a brooding sense of unease.

In the past she had endured several periods of confinement, due to a supposed
weakness of mind. And on many occasions, had suffered dangerous nose-bleeds,
a sign her brain was congested, so the alienists claimed.

In her small house in Esher, she endured a sense of abandon, as her husband,
in service, 'worked in' with the Crown.* Alone for weeks, she sought solace in
company; one man in particular, from outside the town.

But before it began, the deception had failed; Brough's husband had her
followed by Henry Field, an amateur sleuth. When he reported his findings
the next morning, Brough's marriage was over and he knew what to do.
Confronting Mary with the truth, he declared that he would break up their
home; proceedings for divorce would begin the next day.

True to his word, he contacted Mary and explained there was a document
she was expected to sign. As well as calling an end to their ruinous marriage, he
would keep all those children still living at home.

The Most Awful of Crimes

Now facing life on her own, with no fiscal arrangements, Mary Ann Brough
concocted a plan. In the early hours of the morning, the day before her husband

---

* At Claremont, a mile from Esher, occupied then by the exiled French royal family.

was due with his papers, she cut the throats of the children with dreadful effect. Completing the deed, she turned her own throat to the razor, intending to bring all the pain to an end.

A few hours later, two workmen, Woolgar and Peastly,* were passing the cottage when they raised the alarm. A bloodstained pillow was draped from the window and, though they saw movement, they could not get inside. Procuring a ladder, Woolgar climbed up to the bedroom – and was met by a scene of unimaginable hell. As he watched, Mary Brough came forward from the top of the stairs:

> 'her throat was cut, and her hands and face were covered with blood, and her hair hung about her face. She [made] a whistling noise, apparently from the wound' (*JPM* 7: 609).

Escaping back down the ladder, he bellowed at Peastly to race for the doctor, and to tell the constable he was needed as well. Within minutes, all four had climbed through the window – but nothing had prepared them for the horror they saw.

William, so young, lay unnaturally 'sleeping'; in the next room they entered, they discovered two more children. Stretched out on the bed, lying beside them, Mary reached out her arm in a pitiful plea. In a third room, they found the other three children; undressed for the night-time, but dead to the world. They had uncovered *six* blatant murders – but was Mary the culprit or a victim of crime?

A stream of people soon flooded the building: doctors, neighbours, the local police. Dr Mott, who had previously treated the suffering woman, stitched the wound in her throat. Now, at least, she could talk.

In the company of Police Superintendent Biddlecomb, she began her confession – though he repeatedly warned her not to say something she might later regret. She had no motive to offer, no justification, but she referred to a menacing darkness that had clouded her thoughts. She had, she said, committed the murders, while under its hold and quite out of sorts. But was this, her account, in any way truthful, or was she simply preparing the insanity plea?

---

* As recorded in *JPM* 7: 609.

Too Much of a Trial

On 9 August, at Guildford Assizes, defence counsel duly claimed that Mary was mad. As 'proof', they pointed to her previous confinements, a history of temporary paralysis brought on by her womb. The alienists called it a *catamenial madness*, while her attacks coincided with her 'time of the month'.

Forbes B. Winslow (*see Part 1*), a critical witness, said her insanity rose from a disease of the brain. Previous and ongoing struggles had altered its structure – if they only had means and the chances to see.

He went on to explain how 'transient (or temporary) insanity' frequently resulted in homicidal attacks. A controversial assertion, brought on by *irresistible impulse*, and only made famous by its frequent rejection in law.

Future and worsening illness was indefinitely certain; the black cloud she referred to suggested impending attack. What's more, he concluded, it was often accompanied, by a suicidal desire to bring death to themselves. And to lasting effect, he confirmed assaults of this nature, often occurred between a mother and child.

Prosecution

For others, such 'clap-trap' would never pardon the horror – *blocked menstruation* had no pretext in law (though *see also Brixey – Part 5*). Responding to a rise in public disquiet, prosecution counsel went to town on their point.

Mrs Brough was *not* mad, she was a conniving, obstinate slattern! Hers was no temporary insanity, it was murder pre-planned. With malice aforethought, the premeditated murders were a wicked response to her jealous tirade. On the eve of her husband bringing round divorce papers, she revealed her true self as someone depraved.

At this point, a letter was opened, in which Mary bequeathed the few things of her own. Trinkets and jewellery, some of no little value, she left to her daughter and out of *his* hands.

Depravity *(see Part 2)* – *that* was the 'condition' – brought on by a life of immorality and vice. And now that her husband had wanted the children, she reacted with anger as though it were war.

Brough's was a case that had marked out a battle – between alienists who believed her and those who did not. Such in-fighting was welcome, to the law and its practice, reducing her chances to nothing at all.

Judgement

Mr Justice Erle, lead judge, favoured prosecution's position. He rejected Brough's *irresistible impulse* as a nonsense to most. As far as he was concerned, it had no place in legal proceedings and he directed the jury to dismiss it from mind.

Instead, he concluded, they should find her guilty of murder; despite knowing full well it would lead to her death.

To everyone's surprise, they declared her not guilty, on the ground of insanity affecting her mind. Forbes Winslow, for one, erupted with passion – and later mocked with irony those who had wanted her hanged:

> 'If [Mary Ann Brough] were insane, her mental derangement was the result of the immoral life she had led for years, and as her insanity was self-created, the gallows ought to have claimed her for its victim' (*ibid*: 623).

The Aftermath and Macabre

Brough was sent to Bethlem Hospital where she was due to be held until Her Majesty's Pleasure be known. So great was the interest in her crime and acquittal, tours of her house were sold at a penny a time!

Just eight years on, the 'Esher Murderess' was no longer; she died while still an inmate on the criminal wards. A *post-mortem* revealed what Winslow had propounded: there were clots on her brain. Had it caused the loss of her mind?

Thomas 'Ransome' Collins – *A Known Road to Ruin*

Monday 19 June 1893 – Murder; Delusions, Cardiff
A brutal case from the Welsh capital reveals Victorian attitudes towards both crime and insanity and the sentence of death. A ravenous press, hunting for scandal – a public cry for humanity on the strangest of grounds; the waning belief in the Home Secretary's Mercy – and an insanity plea opposing the Rules.

The Crime
Thomas Collins, 28 years old – known also as 'Ransome' – rushed the two policemen patrolling Bute Terrace on the 'wrong' side of town. A bloodied knife still grasped in his hand, the men listened in horror as he revealed the story of a violent attack. The dead woman's body, he told them, was just a few yards away.

In fact, Mary Sheen, 25, was still clinging on bravely, when PC Green came across her behind Mary-Ann Street. Leaning down, he tried to make out her words, but her voice, like her breathing, was already fading and drifting away.

The other policeman, King, had taken Collins across town to the station, while Green now sent a runner to fetch Dr Roche. By the time the police surgeon arrived, she had lost her fight with the living, though the blood was still seeping from her multiple wounds.

Collins' (Recent) Behaviour
Before his life fell apart, Thomas Collins had been a respectable fireman (stoker), serving his time on the ships leaving port. Indeed, his grief-stricken mother confirmed he was never as happy than when messing on boats and far out to sea.

His relationship with Mary, once started, had always been violent. Yet for two years, they had shared houses spread across town. Time after time he moved out, going back to his mother; and time after time agreed to 'one final go'.

It could not have helped that Mary was married [her real name was Sweeney], though she always lived life as if she were not. Taking a number of lovers – whether for money or pleasure? – Collins had never accepted she was one he must share.

A Lead up to Murder
Only nine days before the murder, Collins had been released from the prison, after serving six months for stealing some shoes. But at least Mary was waiting

as the gates were thrown open – though there were many who thought this would only bring woe.

Both staying at his mother's, on Herbert Street in the town, he soon confronted Mary about a lie she had told. He and his mother had *never* been lovers; how could she utter such a sickening claim? In his temper he felled her and followed in with his boot. All the while she denied it, as his mother looked on.

By the following Friday, 16 June, he met Mary's half-sister, appearing greatly excited: 'I will do for her [Mary], and have the rope [if I must]!' He headed off to her dwelling in Mary-Ann Street.

By the Saturday evening they were lovers again, this time at her house, the future scene of the crime. Unsurprisingly, violence erupted, which left a gash in her cheek that had to be sewn. [The attendant at the Royal Infirmary recalled the woman once he heard of the murder.]

Yet again, Collins returned to his mother, but on Monday went back to Mary, a pivotal day he would come to regret.

Gruesome details of the murder were seized upon, both by the press and the locals … Collins, it seemed, had entered the house, this time armed with a knife. 'I will kill you, Mary, and die like a man!' were the last words he spoke before his frenzied attack.

The first swipe nicked her vein, on the right of the neck. Others brought death ever closer, though they were never the cause. His *thirteenth* lunge, however – the one that eventually killed her – had, by luck or design, ripped through her heart.

Yet Mary still managed to run out to the yard and, in a desperate attempt at escape, tried to scale the wall. With life ebbing away, she fell onto the paving, hitting the spot where she would stay until found. The wall was later described, in the reports in the papers, as 'covered with the poor woman's lifeblood', so bad were her wounds.

A Hard Case to Answer

On 4 August, the trial at Glamorgan Assizes was held in Swansea, fifty miles away. So strong – and widespread – was the sense of excitement, the doors to the court were closed early to stifle the crowds.

An Insanity Plea?

Unusually, it was Williams, prosecution counscl, who raised the possibility Collins might be insane. Though, he reminded the jury, the onus to diagnose madness and prove any plea remained with the defence (though cf *Davies et al, Part 5*).

Lewis, for the defence, interjected at once. He thought Thomas Collins was undeniably mad. He claimed the poor man had been suffering *delusions* – their subject: the dead woman's unsavoury claims. It thus followed, he continued, by some natural extension, it was for the prosecution to prove she had spoken the lie. If not, then it must be his client's unhealthy invention, that he had been driven mad by a trick of the brain.

Presiding judge, Justice Charles, was visibly shaken. He rejected the assertion that delusions could exonerate crime.

Lewis continued there was no doubting his client, he had definitely committed the terrible crime. But the jury should reason, not on whether he did it, but on whether he was ever in a sound state of mind. With one eye on the Bench, and no doubt trying to be clever, he asked whether Collins had known a right from a wrong.

'Alienist' Witness

Leading up to the trial, vague references in the press, to Collins' dubious madness, spoke of liquor in the minutes ahead of the crime. These were 'proved' – it was claimed – when he declined a friend's invitation to enter the pub and find solace in drink. In truth, it was how he rejected the notion that mattered more than the decision itself: a vacant stare had been followed by a curious statement: 'The train has not yet come', was all he had said.

Rumours had since circulated that Collins was never right in his thinking, since he came out of gaol only a few days before. He would, people said, run up to a stranger, shake their hand, wish them good day and then tear off his coat.

Others reported a long-term change in his manner: having once been so 'tidy' and having 'worked' for his keep. Everything changed when 'he fell in with [that] woman', a fact duly confirmed by his mother at home.

More recent had been his demeanour in prison: as he awaited his hearing, he had said he would die. Allegations were made that he wanted to appear undefended – to remove any 'danger' that he should escape with his life.

Three witnesses were called – the prison's governor and doctor, and the surgeon who attended the scene of the crime. All testified to the presence of madness – though none were qualified to make such a claim.

Finally, an hereditary illness was suggested: his father had been 'queer' and drowned himself in the docks. His sister was wont to 'take leave of her senses', though that was brought on when she 'took a sip of the vine'. Two of his cousins (again both paternal) were known to have stayed in the asylum in town. One was now dead, the other still living, with no chance of rescue from his dangerous mind.

At last, an alienist was summoned – hearsay was one thing, expertise something else. Dr Pringle, Superintendent of Bridgend Asylum, was much more precise [though, in truth, only just].

During two interviews with Collins, he heard he had been mad with a fever, while stationed abroad – in Jaffa, he thought. Now seemingly unafraid of his own (imminent?) passing, Pringle said this proved Collins was a dangerous fool.

Pringle was adamant – Collins suffered delusions – and concluded he was mad at the time of his crime. But then he evoked considerable surprise, by quickly suggesting, that though he was troubled, he was no risk to the town! [The assumed reference to the removed cause of his madness – ie Mary – was never reported, and none has been found.]

When Williams [prosecution] suggested that Collins had known right from wrong – having said at the time he would 'die like a man' [ie, he expected the gallows] – Pringle insisted it proved nothing at all. He might well have understood the cold repercussions, but he had still not accepted what he did had been *wrong*.

No Other Choice
As Justice Charles now summed up the trial, he reminded the jury of a number of things. Delusions *per se* were no defence in the courtroom; unless they removed the defendant's awareness that the action committed was legally wrong.

The jury took half-an-hour to find Collins guilty of murder. The foreman declined when asked to say more. The judge accepted the decision and moved to pass sentence; adding there could have been no other outcome, as far as he thought.

Media Frenzy

The local *Western Mail* now went to town, not just with the murder, but the whole sordid affair. Day after day, over so many columns, they reported the prospects for Collins' fate. On the national pages, attention was ruthless. The *Illustrated Police News* splashed the case as its lead.

The victim herself received raucous polemic, as her life was revealed as a one of moral decay. The company she kept was being a clear example – such as the drunken young housemate who slept through the murder – until being woken much later by the press and police!

Final Say

Thomas Collins awaited the gallows, spending thirteen full days on Cardiff Prison's death row. But from the moment the jury had delivered its verdict, efforts were made to gain a reprieve.

The insatiable press continued reporting – but at least one [*Western Mail*] now appeared to have taken his side. '[W]e are glad to learn,' they stated, that a petition for the Home Secretary's Mercy was, as they wrote, 'being extensively signed'. [Signatories included members of the council and even the mayor.]

However, his date of execution was now set for Monday 21 August, and Collins' fortunes looked increasingly bleak. Then, on the Friday before, came a letter from London; it was set out in the press the very next day:

> *Sir, – With reference to your letter of the 13th instant, as to the mental condition of Thomas Collins, now in the prison at Cardiff, having been sentenced to death, I am directed by the Secretary of State to acquaint you that a special medical inquiry has been held into the mental condition of the convict, and that, in view of all the circumstances of the case, the Secretary of State has advised her Majesty to respite the capital sentence, with a view to the removal of the convict to the Broadmoor Criminal Lunatic Asylum.*
>
> > *I am, sir, your obedient servant,*
> > *GODFREY LUSHINGTON.*
> > > (*Western Mail*, 19 August 1893)

Thomas Collins was saved – though perhaps not to his liking! As it transpired his transfer to Broadmoor had already been made.

Thomas & Mary Cruse – *The Evils of Drink*

Tuesday 5 June 1838 – Attempted Murder; Automatism (whilst drunk), Thatcham, Berkshire

Thomas Cruse and his wife Mary, some eleven years his senior, were charged with attacking 7-year-old Charlotte Heath – Mary's daughter from an earlier affair. The offence, at the couple's home on Stroud Green in Thatcham, captured public opinion – as much for the trial as the criminal deed. Had the pair shown intent to murder the child, or had drink left them mad enough to plead common assault? Not for the first time, the evils of drink poured scorn on the insanity debates.

The Crime

On 5 June 1838, Thomas Cruse came home from the tavern and begged his wife, Mary, for more money for drink. Though herself very drunk, she flatly refused. Closing the street door behind him, a bestial 'rumpus' caused their neighbour, Frances Alder, to yet again fear for their miserable lives. Unable to ignore the sounds of merciless violence, she felt sick to the stomach as the fighting grew worse.

At length, she could hear that a silence had fallen; followed quickly by Thomas Cruse leaving the house. His voice tore through the air, as he summoned the terrified Charlotte, who had cowered outside away from the fight.

The girl pleaded: 'Father, do not beat me.' But faced with his thunder, she went meekly inside.

Alder was frantic – all she could hear was the child getting hurt.

Then a voice, Mary – the girl's own 'loving' mother:

'You can beat her. Beat her. Whenever you want!'

Crushing sounds of brutality, before Mary's voice came again:

'Kill her! Kill her! I won't come near you [make a complaint] if you kill her!'

Alder imagined the blows raining down.

At last, the girl ran from the house with blood on her clothing. Mary caught hold of her hand and dragged her inside. Without closing the door, she gave her daughter a beating, smacked the side of her head and pushed her to him.

An eternity passed, and then only silence – the beating, at last, had come to an end. Seconds later, Mary's voice, now shriller than ever, conveyed the absolute horror that Alder had known:

'Murder! Murder! My child is murdered!'

Frances Alder raced round to the cottage, to find the woman cradling the girl. The young body hung limp, she was clearly unconscious as the blood leaked from her ears and fell from the mouth.

Alder snatched the poor child – she was fetching a doctor – and sent a neighbour off running to get the police.

Unfortunate Witness
In the course of three visits, Carter, the Newbury surgeon, never once saw the girl recover and wake. Her concussion, he confirmed, was 'an injury dangerous to life'. [Though readers will be relieved to know she came round in the end.]

A young girl called Fanny Bradley had witnessed the beating through the open front door after Charlotte's escape (and recapture by Mary). She confirmed how Thomas had struck her, his hands and feet as his weapons, before throwing her down on the floor and smashing her head on a beam.

Only then had his wife collapsed in hysterics.

A month later, the couple stood trial at the Berkshire Assizes. Both indictments were as lengthy as they were flowery in words. In short, they were charged with *attempting to murder*:

'The jurors for our Lady the Queen upon their oath, present that Thomas Cruse, late of the parish of Thatcham, in the county of Berks aforesaid, labourer, not having the fear of God before his eyes, but being moved and seduced by the instigation of the devil, on the 5th day of June, in the first year of the reign of our Sovereign Lady Victoria ... with force and arms ... in and upon one Charlotte Heath, feloniously, wilfully, and of *his malice aforethought*, did maliciously make an assault ... and that the said T.C. then and there feloniously did cause unto the said C.H. *a certain bodily injury dangerous to the life of her* the said C.H." (8 *C&P*: 541, my *emphasis*).

While Mary was charged separately with:

'aiding, abetting, and assisting the said T.C.... to do and commit contrary to the form of the statute in such case made and provided' (*ibid*).

On Trial – But For What?

The exact form of words foretold an impending confusion. It wasn't enough to gain the right sort of outcome, the law would soon fail to agree the right kind of charge.

Carrington, for the defence, immediately issued a pair of *demurrers* – legal objections – designed, in effect, to question *intent*: 'however violent the conduct of the prisoners had been, they had formed no intention of murdering the child' (*ibid*: 545).

He invoked three separate debates:

- was the act common assault or attempted murder?
- which of the two had carried out the attack?
- and what part had drink* played in the awful affray?

First, he challenged the legality of the long-winded charges – they included no outcome (ie, whether the victim had died); or whether the accused had <u>intended</u> to murder. If neither, they must be tried on common assault.

Secondly, he said, it ignored Mary's right to a legal presumption: that her husband coerced her to the criminal act![†]

These points – and the many others that followed – would protract the proceedings for almost eight months.

---

* Alienists had made much of the effects of hard drinking – was it now worthy of pardon through the insanity plea (*see Part 2*)?

The original trial was allowed to continue after the judge, Justice Patteson, struck an unusual deal. He assured Carrington that an inquiry would follow the end of proceedings, any sentence wiped clean if it thought the indictments were false.

Cruse's counsel agreed.

A Short (Doubtful) Defence

There now remained a chance of the plea of insanity. That, if the defendants were found guilty of anything, had drunkenness effected the act? Patteson paused and was forced to consider, though this time arrived at a view of his own.

Reminding the jury that drunkenness was no exculpatory matter – *other than its relationship to the malicious intent* – he turned to the jury with particular relish:

> '[A]lthough drunkenness is no excuse in any crime *whatever*, it is often of very great importance in cases where it is a question of intention. A person may be so drunk as to be utterly unable to form any intention and yet he may be guilty of very great violence' (*ibid*: 546).

If accepted as a chronic condition – in insanity terms, *automatism*, meaning out of control (*see Part 2*) – then that again would infer there had been no intention – because drunkenness had negated the means to control such a thought. An insanity verdict could still lead to the accused being detained at Her Majesty's Pleasure.

Aside from the drink, such intent [to commit murder] might be thought of as lacking if no *fatal injury* were attempted or 'shown to be tried' [a point not lost in Carrington's challenge]. In short, for the more serious charge – attempting to murder – it was necessary to show there had been the intent to cause death. If that was unlikely – from either the *absence* of injury or indeed the *presence* of drink – then assault was the charge the defendants should face.

The jury were reeling.

Having heard harrowing accounts of the violence in question, their verdict revealed just how uncertain they were. Three issues – premeditated violence, harmful intent, and exculpatory drinking – appeared wrongly conflated as the foreman declared. Both defendants were guilty ... but of common assault. Each was imprisoned, the term to be set.

Post-Trial Inquiry

On 17 November, staying true to his word, Patteson empanelled an inquiry into the tone of the charge. *Fifteen* judges reviewed the indictment, and struggled to answer the problems it posed.

At first, they agreed a series of questions:

- had the accused *intended* to murder the victim?
- had her injuries been enough to *prove* that intent – that is, had the act deliberately 'inflict[ed] injury dangerous to life'?
- had the indictment wording addressed those two questions?
- if the charge had remained (attempting to murder), had Mary Cruse been afforded her right to plead her duress?[†]

Drawing frequently on case history, often from trials that had limited bearing, they struggled to fashion a reasoned reply. By way of example, grievous bodily harm (thought a comparable charge) was stated in law to be plainly less vague:

'A man (*sic*) may intend to do grievous bodily harm without having any specific intent as to what the harm should be, and he may not care much whether he injures the other person on the head or the body' (*ibid*: 549).

In other words, if the Cruses had been charged with GBH, even with no malice aforethought, it was enough they should be found guilty and punished as charged. But theirs was not GBH, it could yet still be an intention to murder. But it remained the more serious charge on which they *failed to agree*.

Now the argument was in danger of going full circle. And at the last the judges spied a clever way out. To avoid the risk of either defendant escaping conviction, the decision was reached – it was *common assault*. This way, both were liable to the felony charged.

The original trial sentences were dutifully sanctioned, the Cruses would each spend a term in the gaol. He was given nine months, but she just the one. And it seems from the records that poor Charlotte stayed home.

[†] Turning instead to the issue of Mary's unspoken claims of her husband's coercion, a wife was 'entitled' to follow that line of defence (236 ER: 22) [reformed in 1925]. But it should only apply in the then three capital cases: murder, attempted murder and treason as well.

David Davies the Elder – *Unfit To Plead*

Monday 9 August 1852 – Murder; Unfit to Plead, Oldswinford, Worcestershire
Standing trial for the murder of Mary Pardoe, David Davies the Elder, 47,
became the *victim* of two inter-related debates. First, should the defendant
have automatic representation (ie defence counsel)? And second, who bore the
'burden of proof' (*see Glossary*) that he was fit to stand trial?

A Lucky Defendant?
Defence counsel, if the accused had the money, was regular practice since
1836. The law took its course for those who had not. By the time David
Davies appeared, he could count himself lucky: the courts supplied free legal
representation, at least in capital cases when the sentence was death.

   Ascertaining 'fitness to plead' was a different dilemma: the defence bore
the onus to show they were mad. But trials had been heard where the Crown had
been ordered to prove they were, in fact, sane enough to stand trial.

   Confusingly, for a time, both options existed. It made the 'burden of proof'
another lottery to win.

'A Dreadful Occurrence'
At the Seven Stars public house, in the Worcestershire village of Oldswinford,
a number of navvies were causing trouble outside. The atmosphere had been
sour, and threatened to worsen, prompting Davies, the landlord, to career into
the crowd thrashing out with his stick. The mob soon ran for cover, only to
reform at the moment he left. He decided that he had only one option.

   On his heels, he marched back inside and made straight for the stairs. Within
seconds, he approached the middle upstairs room window, threw it up on its
sash and lifted his arms. Looking down, he aimed the double-barrelled shotgun
he kept for protection, and unloaded a shot deep into the crowd.

   'I've given them one sweep,' he declared. 'Now I'll give them another…!'
And fired again as screams filled the air. 'Here's into you, you bastards!'

   Mary Pardoe, mother of six and a labourer's wife, succumbed in an instant;
others lay hurt as he went back inside. Seconds later again, he was back at the
window – and fired off two more shots into the crowd. Still not content, he
repeated the action, though this time a window was blown from its frame! As
the policeman came running, the 'madman' stopped firing. David Davies the
Elder was under arrest.

Worcester Assizes, 12 March 1853

Davies showed little concern for the one he had murdered, or for his own fatal position as he stood in the court. Two days after the shooting, on the 11 August, he was indicted for trial at the magistrate's court. It would take time to appear at the local Assizes – it was seven long months before he arrived in the dock.

When he did, he was said to have entered in quite 'a strange manner', before adopting the silence of an unfortunate mute. When repeatedly asked to submit to his standing, he responded at length in the following way:

'I have not killed anybody; they didn't come to fight; I was to fight, but I haven't seen them yet' (6 *Cox C C*: 326).

The jury were asked if they were the words of a madman or, as Allen suggested, he was putting it on … Mr Allen, prosecution serjeant (*sic*), observed that feigning insanity was a popular ploy. He reminded the court it was defence counsel's sworn duty to prove he was not, at that moment, fit to enter his plea.

Huddlestone (defence) argued he was very mistaken; citing statute devised during the reign of King George (40 Geo. III, c. 94, s. 2). He pointed out that a new jury should surely be entered and try, if the defendant was fit to proceed .

Allen cried out – that was Huddlestone's onus! But Huddlestone maintained it was for Allen to prove. In making his point, Huddlestone enforced the opinion that men were presumed innocent until guilt had been shown. Allen, he said, must prove when the defendant is guilty – the same should apply to his fitness to plead.

Unsurprising Confusion

The impasse they reached was in no way surprising … the debate had drawn inconsistent responses before. In the past, when defendants were shown to be physically unable (ie *dumb*), a 'not guilty' plea was recorded at court. But then Davies the Elder had proved he *was* able – only what he had said made no sense at all!

The judge, Mr Justice Vaughan Williams, struggled to reach a decision – and what he came up with unsettled the law. *If the prosecution could not ascertain proof of the defendant's sanity, then he must first try to secure it outside the court.*

He called both sides to his intimate chambers, where he also summoned the gaoler and prison medical staff. When they reappeared in court, David Davies the Elder was placed again at the bar as the jury filed past.

Once again, he was asked to enter a plea, and once again he stood upright but perfectly mute. So Vaughan Williams read out his pre-agreed dictum: the jury should try first whether Davies was *sane*.

Vaughan Williams ordered Allen to start – to call witnesses to prove the trial could proceed. So the same gaoler and doctors were separately brought forward – but to the dismay of the court, they were unable to say!

Now Huddlestone stood up, but he fared little better, declaring an absence of witnesses who could prove the man *mad*. This, he assured them, was because he'd had no time to unearth them – seven months was apparently not enough.

Vaughan Williams despaired; they were no further forward. And with the defendant still standing he summed up for court:

'[W]hile on the one hand it would be a serious thing to put a man on his trial, when incapable of properly instructing his counsel for his defence, yet on the other hand, the jury should carefully guard against giving prisoners the opportunity, by simulating madness, to pervert the course of justice even for a single day' (6 *Cox C C*: 328).

He then reminded the jury of their right to a judgement, to declare on the accused's current state of his mind. Only *they* could decide on the troublesome issue – was David Davies the Elder fit to enter a plea?

The jury retired, but were back in an instant; in their humble opinion: no, he was not.

The judge insisted Davies be kept at Her Majesty's Pleasure (*see Glossary*), while further inquiries took place outside court. His move to adjourn was placed on the record, but no reference was made to when they should all reconvene.

An Unusual Outcome
The chances of Davies ever returning to trial had been shown over history to be exceptionally slim. Such 'insane on arraignments' were often conveniently forgotten, the prisoner's charge seldom heard from again.

Yet, on 12 July – some three years later – he was brought back to court to stand trial again. Presenting a man now recovered from his earlier sickness, Davies entered his plea: 'Not guilty' as charged.

Now a new point of order was quickly presented – Huddlestone had struck a deal with his opponents in law. In exchange for admission of guilt in the matter, a charge of *manslaughter* meant the case should be shelved.

The judge, Baron Alderson (*see Part 1*), in charge of the hearing, said he could never accept such a turn of events. The trial, he insisted, would proceed as was proper – the murder charge stood, and Davies entered his plea.

With a new jury sworn in, prosecution counsel (Mr Best) was the first at the lectern – but he offered no evidence in support of the charge. With the hearing now over – David Davies 'not guilty' – a new charge of manslaughter was entered instead.

Not Quite the End

Having waited three years for his plea to the charges, he now gave his second in less than an hour. In a voice clear and strong, with no sign of his madness, he turned to the jury: 'Guilty,' he said.

Baron Alderson moved immediately to sentence, but with it he delivered a further surprise. He was of the opinion that, had the first trial proceeded, the same verdict – manslaughter – should have been made at the time.

In ordering the defendant to spend two years in prison, he agreed Davies had fired in a fit of extreme 'irritation'. He also doubted the prisoner would spend the full term.

William Dove – *'Bad boy … bad man'*

Monday 25 February to Saturday 1 March 1856 – Poisoned His Wife; ?
Moral Insanity, Leeds

Few cases drew greater attention – nor better summed up the crime and insanity debates – than that of 'the poisoner', 35-year-old William Dove. Following the death of his wife, amidst scandal and rumour, he faced claims of consorting with wizards, unbelievable cruelty and cavorting with Satan – in equal amount!

His insanity plea spoke of three separate 'conditions': *imbecility, defective intellect* and *moral insanity* – the latter being the most controversial of all. Such claims proved too much for the judge, Baron Bramwell – who preferred the jury's opinion to medical 'truths'.

Several alienists – including Bucknill and Winslow – asserted Dove's curious behaviour would be found in his past.

Background

Dove's 'depraved' conduct began when still only a boy. Aged 7, he stripped naked, cut himself with a knife and signed his letters in blood. He also used the household supply of candles and wax to summon up spirits and commune with the dead. He later used them to set light to his room.

Around the same time, ensuring the poker glowed orange, he chased his sister around while he threatened to brand her.

When just 12 years old, he acquired a pistol, and proudly told school friends it was to murder his father – that he would finish him off before he went out to work.

As a farmer's apprentice – a position secured by his desperate family – he burnt the animals with 'oil of vitriol', and seared out their eyes. Even the wife of the farmer encountered his 'evil' – as he showed her the knife to be used when her husband returned.

All the while, he retained his interest in supernatural happenings – a thing he put to some use when faced with losing his home. In 1854, given notice to quit the farm he had only recently rented, he changed his mind once the deal was agreed. Employing Henry Harrison, a 'wise-man (more of him later) he sought to 'enchant' the farm steward into allowing him back. Despite this, he complained of troublesome spirits, and goblins who made him afraid to go home.

All this and more – much too disturbing to publish – would be brought out at his trial, when he was finally 'caught'. To either be used as proof of his madness, or confirming his guilt as a monster depraved.

A Slow Death to the End

Harriet Dove [William's long-suffering wife] had apparently felt ill for a very long time. But the week recently started would by far be her worst.

Monday 25 February

Following breakfast, she played the pianoforte a little, before offering to help Elizabeth Fisher, the servant, make up the beds. However, while climbing the stairs, her legs seemed to fail her, leaving her stranded and frightened as she called out for help.

Presenting all the signs of a panic-struck husband, William helped move her to a chair in her room. Sending Fisher next door – for Mrs Witham, the neighbour – she was quick to come round, as he had hoped that she would.

By the time Harriet's physician, Dr Morley, was informed of her trouble, he was unable to visit but would send someone else. A young man named Scarth arrived before lunchtime, and recorded her symptoms as nothing he'd known:

> 'I found her complaining of pain in her chest. Her fingers were clenched
> into the palms of her hands; her jaws were closed; and her muscles were
> twitching. The head was slightly thrown back, and the shoulders likewise.
> Her feet and legs were stretched out straight' (Williams 1856: lvi).

Her limbs, he corrected, were not only twitching; by some uncontrollable means, they were thrashing around. While her breathing was hard, from the pain in her body, and her teeth, for some time, had been permanently clenched.

Relief only came from rubbing her back, which Mrs Witham did now with the liniment he brought. And later, from a medicine sent on by Morley – which attracted intense speculation as her illness progressed.

At 11am on Wednesday 27, Harriet Dove suffered a second attack. The following day, she suffered two more. Then one, at 10.30 on Friday evening, failed to loosen its hold until early next day. The final attack – some twelve hours later – at last proved too much for the woman to bear.

An Arresting Post-Mortem

After concerns voiced by his pupils – Scarth and another, named Elletson – Morley decided a *post-mortem* should be done. Both had confessed to supplying strychnine to William, apparently to get rid of some troublesome cats.*

The symptoms displayed had been consistent with poison, but he proceeded with caution before sharing his thoughts. When he dissected the late woman's stomach, he found enough of the poison to know it was the cause of her death.

On Friday 7 March, Dove was arrested on suspicion of murder.

[Any casual suspicions that Dove had deliberately administered the poison were formalised when Morley had insisted the *post-mortem* be held. As the court would soon hear, it was the one outcome Dove feared most – telling Morley that Harriet herself would have morally objected.

It was later deduced that he had administered six doses of increasing proportions – to make her death more gradual, as though she were ill.]

Trial and Plea

On 16 July, at his trial in York Castle, an account of William Dove's past was presented to court. Testimony was given by so many who knew him – 'clergymen, dissenting ministers, schoolmasters, farmers, and servants, male and female' (Williams 1856: 14), most of them recounting a difficult life (*see introduction*).

Overend (lead prosecutor) outlined the effects that strychnine could have. In describing its use as a murderer's weapon, he labelled the deed as the worst of its kind: '[It was] one of the most cold-blooded and cruel murders almost known in the history of crime' (*ibid*: xviii).

Comparing Harriet's symptoms to those seen in cases of tetanus and hysteria, he first dismissed the former by the order of things. Both illnesses – tetanus and poisoning by strychnine – bore similar symptoms, but they showed themselves differently in the build-up to death.

Nor, he continued, was hysteria likely. As Scarth (Morley's pupil) now said: 'Some of the symptoms were symptoms of hysteria, as I believe; but as a whole they were not' (*ibid*: lvii).

He concluded on a point of no doubt: Harriet Dove had died from ingesting strychnine.

[*See Appendix 4* for his fuller report]

He then offered the jury three possible *motives* – such things, he knew, would thwart the insanity plea. First, having a long history of illness, Harriet had caused Dove a great deal of expense. Second, she had blighted his affection by plaguing him endlessly to desist from his errant behaviour (drinking and women?). Third – and perhaps the one most contentious – he harboured intentions to make Mrs Witham his wife!

Dove's acquisition of strychnine, he then claimed, took place on three separate occasions. Each had been obtained from Dr Morley's own rooms [this was not known by the medic until after Harriet's death]. The first two quotas – some 10 grains and six grains respectively [note: one-and-a-half grains was considered enough to murder] – were used as implied to poison some cats. The third, however – of an unknown amount – Dove illicitly took when left all alone. *This*, Overend conjectured, was the supply used in the killing.

Dove's culpability was further suggested when he was heard chastising Harriet for curbing his ways: 'Never you mind,' he said, 'mind your own business, or I'll give you a pill that will do for you.' So alarmed was she, that she begged Fisher, the servant, to offer her word: 'Elizabeth, if I die at any time and you are away from me, it is my wish that you should tell my friends to have my body examined!' (*ibid*: xxiii)[†]. [This, of course, was in direct opposition to the claims made by Dove.] And further betrayed his supposed nefarious fears by asking whether small amounts of poison could be detected that way.

Careless or Clever?
In the days leading up to Harriet's death, even those preceding suspicion, Dove was shown either to have panicked or been incredibly wise. As the prosecution now claimed, he enacted a series of alibis, designed both to cover his guilt, and show him as kind. Several conversations were held with a good number of people, ranging wildly from 'innocent' inquiries to 'careless' remarks.

During the week of her illness, Dove let slip to a servant that his wife was dying and he would be free to re-marry. Dr Morley recalled another similar case: three days before death, he chided the man for insisting his wife was then dying, even though to the medic there were no obvious signs.

His most outlandish predictions, however, came ahead of her attack at 10.30 on Friday (29 February), when he stated the minute the next attack would descend.

In court, it was unclear whether he had been careless or smart.

The Unreliable Wizard

One of the more unsettling inquiries now focussed on his friendship with Henry Harrison (the 'wise-man'), who the press had retitled a wizard to fear. The self-proclaimed soothsayer –'I am a dentist, water-caster and have done a little astrology' – reported how Dove had pursued a discussion about a recent, similar case. William Palmer, the 'Rugeley Poisoner', had been hanged for several murders – after administering strychnine in fatal amounts. Critically his wife, Ann, was thought by some to be one of his victims.

Harrison then recalled how Dove had first approached him, wanting to discuss the supernatural realm. And how, during those early exchanges, he claimed Harrison had foretold Harriet's demise:

'He [Dove] had told me that he sold his soul to the devil, but he thought I had greater power over the devil than [any] himself.'

He added:

'[that] I could send the devil to frighten his wife'.

Much later, he claimed, Dove had insisted he read from the *Mercury* newspaper, detailing Palmer's own methods and the effects of his crime.

He finally alleged that Dove had asked him whether *he* could get him some strychnine – to which the 'wizard' responded:

'Not for the world!'
'If you won't,' Dove responded, 'I will get some somewhere else'.

(*ibid*: li)

Harrison's accounts were undeniably harmful – though he finished by offering Dove a way out. Remembering how he was summoned in the days after Harriet's departure, he recounted the meeting and what had been said:.

'[Dove] gave me a funeral card of his wife, and said there was an inquest over her.
    I said "What for?"

He said, "Can they detect a grain or a grain and a half of strychnia (*sic*)?"

"Why, have you given her some?"

He said, "No, but I got some from Mr Morley's young man, and some may have been spilt, and she might have got some.'"

(*ibid*: l)

Dove's Defence and the Insanity Plea

Dove's barrister, Mr Bliss, strived to rescue his client from what were surely the jaws of defeat. In so doing, he appeared both contradictory and adversely confused.

First he argued for Dove's *innocent* sanity (that is, he had *not* given the poison) then, without pause, for his exculpable *in*sanity (ie accepting he had). But defining a condition would prove much harder to grasp.

An event in Dove's life was put forward as 'proof' of his madness – his father had enquired at the asylum about what to do with the boy. While back in the present, he spoke of the defendant's obsession, and a desire to mimic, what Palmer had done:

'[With] insanity, the impulse to imitation is [thus] irresistible…' (*ibid*: lxxiii)

As well as confirming alienist opinion – that copycat killings were the work of the mad – it was perhaps an attempt to introduce *irresistible impulse*, a more controversial condition when mentioned in court (*see Part 2*).

Extending it further, Bliss began reading, from alienist tracts on conditions he 'suffered' – in particular, Prichard's *moral insanity* (*see Part 2*), the most controversial of all. Critically, he added, it needed no mental delusions – but on this, judge Baron Bramwell said he was going too far.

No less than three medical witnesses were called to give evidence. Among them Caleb Williams, Medical Superintendent of the famed York Retreat. He examined Dove two days before and declared him not in his senses; or, more accurately, 'of unsound mind'.

He listed his 'proof' with the following features:

- a commitment to the supernatural world;
- a feeble power of mind;

- delusions (for example, having sold his soul to the Devil);
- his imitativeness [of Palmer]
- finding a target for otherwise lunatic thoughts (his cruelty to animals when still barely a boy);
- his own (written) declaration of *sanity* (*see below*);
- and *a form of* irresistible impulse though he knew he was doing a wrong [the latter to circumvent Bramwell's adherence to the M'Naghten Rules]

Controversially, the last was predicated not on sudden behaviour, but on an accrued *propensity* [for insanity], leaving his destructive desires no longer controlled.

On this, Bramwell had stomached enough. 'If a man,' he inquired, 'nourishes any passion until it becomes uncontrollable, that is moral insanity?'

Williams confirmed this was so.

But Bramwell could barely hide his revulsion.

Overend, for the prosecution, rebutted the stance. 'Dr Williams ... [has] propounded ... a doctrine more dangerous to society [than was ever] ... uttered in ... court... [i]f the jury would support that theory, gone was the security of every hearth in the country.'

He then emphasised his lament: 'A man was only to be vicious, and to contemplate his crime for a given period, until it became uncontrollable, and then these gentlemen would say it was insanity, and the greater the criminal the more excusable and the more irresponsible was he.'

With little restraint on his growing annoyance, the barrister quickly reached his conclusion: 'that [Dove] was a bad boy, would lead to the inference that he [is] a bad man.'

The question of insanity, he insisted, should have never arisen!

Also rejecting the insanity motion, Mr Pearce, schoolmaster at York's major prison, read out a letter in which Dove declared himself *sane*:

'Dear Sir, – I am very uneasy about a rumour which is said to be prevalent respecting me about the town of Leeds, that I am or pretend to be insane. I hope that my conduct while in prison will prove the contrary. I hope you will testify to the contrary. The talk of the Queen's pleasure, I can't think of it, when I know I am an innocent man. I ask you to give me your best advice' (*ibid*: lxxxviii).

Others (eg Bucknill) dismissed it as either a cunning piece of inverse deception or, in any case, no proof of a disordered mind.

Non-medical testament came from people Dove had previously known. Indeed, many contacted Bliss out of the blue. Most surprising was Jenkins, Harriet's brother [and husband to William Dove's sister!], who paid his own passage from India to support the defence.

Lamenting his relation's eccentric behaviour, he told how his 'expressions of insanity' had come to wear thin. Such as threatening suicide and other violent explosions; yet remaining an affectionate husband during moments of calm.

He then astounded the jury by revealing his own, and his family's, deductions: that Harriet had died from a hysterical fit!

After five hours oration, Bliss admitted Dove had administered poison. But he referred back to Harrison to show that his client had been under the soothsayer's 'spell'. Foretelling Harriet's imminent death, not only had he [Dove] believed in Harrison's portent, his *weak mind* had led him to ensure it came true.

He further cemented the notion of Harrison's hold on his senses, by referring to two letters Dove wrote in his cell:

'Dear Devil, – If you will get me clear at the assizes, and let me have too enjoyment of life, health, wealth, tobacco, beer, more food and better, my wishes granted, and live till I am sixty, come to me and tell me. And remain your faithful servant, William Dove' (*ibid*).

Dove had signed it in blood. [The second was considered too distressing to be read out in court.]

In closing, Bliss imputed the jury, to decide the fate of *such a madman as thinks he has struck a deal with the Devil.*

Summing Up

Bliss had not bargained with Bramwell as judge ... Betraying his anger, the unwavering baron immediately cautioned the jury:

'[I] hardly [know]which of the errors would be the greater— that of punishing an innocent man, or of allowing a man guilty of so horrible a crime… to escape' (*ibid*: *cviii*).

And directed them to consider three stages of 'proof':

'The prisoner being charged with the crime of wilful murder, and the defence being that he was not guilty, or if guilty that he ought to be acquitted on the ground of insanity, the questions for the jury to consider were [these]—did the deceased die from the administration of strychnia?—was the prisoner the person who administered it?—and was the state of his mind such, when he did it, as to exempt him from the consequences of his act?' (*ibid*).

Completely missing the nuanced dissection of Dove's unsoundness of mind, he restricted the jury's verdict to the familiar stance: did Dove know what he did was morally and legally wrong? Only now he went further than even the Rules had intended, when he denied them the prospect of acquitting the man.

Even if Dove *thought* it not wrong, if he administered poison the law said that it was. He was guilty of murder – whether he knew it or not!

Bramwell summed up for a further six hours, during which he showed no sign of exercising restraint. It seemed both Dove and the alienists were going to suffer; the latter for claiming insight which they had simply made up:

'[I believe] that the Jury [are] as competent to form a correct opinion on matters of this kind (alluding to the question of Dove's insanity) as anybody else'. He added: '[I]t would be better, instead of listening to these speculative opinions, for the jury to decide upon the facts which were detailed before them' (*ibid*: cxiii).

At long last, he ordered the jury to retire. And to consider – that is, *closely* consider – their ultimate verdict.

Verdict
The decision they reached betrayed their utter confusion! They returned ninety minutes later with a most curious phrase:

'Guilty, but we recommend him to mercy on the ground of *defective intellect*' (*ibid*: cxv).

Howls of derision flooded the courtroom ... as Bramwell pronounced the sentence of death.

Controversy and Madness

Dove had been accused of deliberate and systematic poisoning. And of unwavering cruelty over a number of days. No matter how raucous the courtroom had sounded, it was vapid compared to what awaited outside.

A war of words exploded across the world's thundering presses, surpassed only by outrage felt in the alienist camp. For though some thought the jury had acted with courage, others thought their verdict had caused disrepute.

Their first target was the 'condition' decided: *defective intellect* was not even a recognised type. Second, its implied meaning was another conundrum – was Dove an *imbecile* or an *idiot* (*see Part 2*); he couldn't be both?

And yet...

Forbes B. Winslow stood apart from the burgeoning furore; forever a man defined by his failings in court. At first dismissive of an exculpatory illness, he expressed his opinion and with it, his thoughts. After meeting with Morley (the medic) and Barret (Dove's solicitor in charge), he 'diagnosed' Dove as an *imbecile* worthy of pardon; and supported the efforts to gain a reprieve:

> '[Dove's] actions were not merely those of a wicked, vicious, or eccentric man, but they evidently sprung out of a stunted, irregularly developed, congenitally defective, and badly organised brain and mind' (*JPM* 9: 585).

Perhaps revealing his still uncertain position, he suggested a grading in the severity of law. While Dove, as a madman, be spared from the scaffold, he should still spend his life in Her Majesty's gaols [ie he was not mad enough for an asylum].

John Bucknill rejected his opponent's opinion. In particular, his 'condition', and for a very good fact. Dove had harboured a 'degree of foresight, [skill] and cool determination...' (*JMS* 3: 131), which no imbecile could, given their mind. Discounting a raft of 'conditions' – including *moral insanity* – he thought Dove not a madman, but wicked throughout. Proof of his *depravity*, he suggested, was his cruel boyhood behaviour – what he did as a boy he had done as a man:

Prichard's Blue Plaque.
(*Courtesy J. Bentham*)

MILLBROOK HOUSE
Dr. JAMES COWLES PRICHARD
BORN HERE
PHYSICIAN, ANTHROPOLOGIST & LINGUIST
1786 – 1848

MAYOR'S PROJECT
1985-86

GLASGOW ROYAL ASYLUM, GARTNAVEL.

Gartnavel Asylum, Glasgow. (© *The British Library Board*)

THE STRAIT WAISTCOAT.

The Strait Waiscoat. (© *The British Library Board*)

Counsel making their point. (© *The British Library Board*)

THE CONVICT NURSERY AT BRIXTON.

Nursery at Brixton Women's Prison after Mayhew and Binny 1862. (*Cornell University and Internet Archive*)

Newgate Gaol (Allnutt).
(© *The British Library Board*)

Brunel's Hungerford Bridge (Bates). (© *The British Library Board*)

Brixey. (© *David J Vaughan*)

THE ESHER TRAGEDY.

Six Children Murdered by their Mother.

You feeling christians give attention,
Young and old of each degree,
A tale of sorrow I will mention,
Join and sympathise with me;
It's of a sad and dreadful murder,
I shall quickly let you hear,
Which was committed by a mother,
On her six young children dear.

The perpetrator of this murder,
Mary Ann Brough it is her name,
And formerly as you may see,
She nursed the blooming prince of Wales.
But now her days of happiness,
Are vanished like the evening's sun,
Good people all, both great and small,
Reflect upon the deed she's done.

One night she could not rest in slumber,
So her own confession says,
Her little children, six in number,
Thus she took their lives away.
Twas with a sharp and fatal razor,
She committed this foul deed,
And one by one she cut their throats,
Which causes each kind heart to bleed.

The first and eldest whom she murdered,
Sad and dreadful to unfold,
Was a sweet and blooming girl,
Something more than ten years old.
And in her wrath and indignation,
Thus she slew them one by one,
Causing death and desolation,
What on earth could urge it on?

One little pretty boy amongst them,
Of the name of Henry,
He cried aloud with eyes of pity,
'Mother, dear, don't murder me,'
She heeded not his praying tongue,
But like a demon fierce and wild,
'My dear,' said she, 'it must be done,'
And thus she slew her other child.

From bed to bed, and to each chamber,
This wretched woman she did go,
While all around her own dear children,
Streams of crimson blood did flow.
The dreadful sight was most surprising,
To behold these children dear,
How their cruel hearted mother,
Cut their throats from ear to ear.

Oh! what must be the woman's motive,
Did she think she'd done amiss,
Or did she think of death and judgment
To perpetrate a deed like this?
But now the wretch she is committed,
To a prison's gloomy cell,
Where midnight dreams to her will whisper
And her deeds of blood will tell.

Within the prison's massive walls,
What anguish will torment her breast,
When phantoms of her six dear children,
Will disturb her of her rest
Such a sad and dreadful murder,
On record there is no worse,
Committed by a cruel mother,
Once the Prince of Wales' Nurse.

CONFESSION OF THE MURDERESS.

The following confession was made by the murderess, to Mr. Biddlecombe, chief superintendent of the Surrey Constabulary:—"On Friday last, I was bad all day; I wanted to see Mr. Izod, and waited all day. I wanted him to give me some medicine. In the evening I walked about, and afterwards put the children to bed, and wanted to go to sleep in a chair.— About nine o'clock, Georgy (meaning Georgianna) kept calling me to bed. I came up to bed, and they kept calling me to bring them some barley water, and they kept calling me till nearly 12 o'clock. I had one candle lit on the chair—I went and got another, but could not see, there was something like a cloud, and I thought I would go down and get a knife and cut my throat, but could not see. I groped about in master's room for a razor—I could not find one—at last I found his keys, and then found his razor. I went up to Georgy, and cut her first; I did not look at her. I then came to Carry, and cut her. Then to Harry—he said, 'don't mother.' I said, 'I must' and did cut him. Then I went to Bill. He was fast asleep. I turned him over. He never awoke, and I served him the same. I nearly tumbled into this room. The two children here, Harriet and George were awake. They made no resistance at all. I then lay down myself." This statement was signed by the miserable woman.

J. HARKNESS, Printer, 151, Church Street, Preston.

'Broadside Ballad' – Lamenting Mary Ann Brough. (© *The British Library Board*)

192

House of Death, Mary-Ann Street, Cardiff (Collins). (© *Amgueddfa Cymru / National Museum of Wales*)

Berkshire Assizes, Abingdon County Hall (Cruse). (*Reproduced by permission of Reading Central Library*)

Seven Stars Public House, Oldswinford (Davies the Elder). (*Author's Collection*)

Hanged for His 'Crime' (Dove).
(© *The British Library Board*)

The Clappers near Caversham – Where Dyer's Babies Were Found. (*Reproduced by permission of Reading Central Library*)

Amelia Dyer – Britain's Worst Serial Killer? (*Reproduced by permission of Reading Central Library*)

The Terrors of Sleep (Fraser).
(© *The British Library Board*)

'Bridge of Sighs', Chester (Gallop). (© *David J Vaughan*)

Scene of the Murder – Burnham Abbey Farm (Hatto). (*From the Buckinghamshire County Museum collections*)

The New Aylesbury Gaol at Bierton Hill (Hatto). (*From the Buckinghamshire County Museum collections*)

Edinburgh's Notorious Calton Gaol
(Howison). (© *The British Library Board*)

'Madman' and the Monarch – Queen Victoria's Brush with Death (Maclean). (*Reproduced by permission of Reading Central Library*)

Hannah Moore's Inhuman Deed (Allegorical). (© *The British Library Board*)

Northwoods Asylum, Bristol (Pownall). (*Wellcome Library, London (V0012272)*)

Derelict Fisherton House Criminal Lunatic Asylum (Turton). (© *David J Vaughan*)

Amelia G. Snoswell and 'My Alice'? (© *The British Library Board*)

Linton Street houses (Sommer). (© *David J Vaughan*)

A Fatal Meeting of Minds (Westron).
(© *The British Library Board*)

Mad Women, Mad Doctors? Mesmerism Exposed. (*Wellcome Library, London* (*L0034922*))

Daniel Hack Tuke. (*Wellcome Library, London* (*V0005917*))

Forbes B. Winslow. (*Wellcome Library, London* (*V0006318*))

New Bethlem Hospital, St George's Fields, Lambeth. (*Wellcome Library, London* (*V0013727*))

Billiard Room, New Bethlem Hospital. (*Wellcome Library, London* (*V0013738*))

Types of Insanity, Devon County Asylum. (*Wellcome Library, London* (*V0016653*))

Henry Maudsley. (*Wellcome Library, London* (*V0026824*))

Alfred Swaine Taylor. (*Wellcome Library, London* (*V0028432*))

'[Dove's acts] … resemble[d] recklessness, cruelty, and malice, which have been often described as the marks of a depraved boyhood' (*ibid*: 132).

His considered opinion was that Dove should be hanged.

Caleb Williams, who of course spoke at the trial, continued to take a more liberal stance. He believed Dove's insensibility to pain (his own as well as to others) placed 'him beyond the limits of either sanity or responsibility' and thus did not deserve to be cruelly hanged (Williams 1856:16).

Moreover, he saw Dove's obsession with Satan with similar conviction, and believed that Dove's madness was in cumulative form. The man was insane not from a moment, but a *lifetime of moral perversion* expressed over time.

Finally, he castigated Bramwell for entrusting the laymen (ie jury) and not medical experts, to determine Dove's state of mind. And they had shown how misplaced that favour was by declaring conditions that were not even known!

An Ending
On 9 August, attempts at reprieve proved to fall on deaf ears – the nation's most infamous poisoner [after Palmer] was led to the rope. With tales of obsession with supernatural dealings, he was despatched to discover the far side of life.

---

* Strychnine and its effects (*after* Williams 1856) – A plant-poison, extracted by science into a granular substance that causes death with just two grains. Given in small enough doses, however, each passes with no long-term effects (unlike cumulative poisons, such as arsenic). Administered solid or dissolved (as in Harriet's medicine?), it is bitter to taste and takes effect in no more than an hour (often in only a matter of minutes). Once ingested, it requires several factors to work: the amount given, the form when conveyed, amount of food in the stomach, the victim's powers of absorption and whether the stomach contents are acid or alkaloid at the time. Its symptoms include: great pain, muscle spasms and internal organ decay, yet it has no effect on the sufferer's brain. Indeed, the victim remains perfectly conscious, as did Harriet Dove when she experienced pain. Death finally comes from a terrifying asphyxia, as the lungs cease to function and the patient is unable to breathe.

† As for administering the poison, Harriet herself had long suspected her husband. The attacks, each having gradually subsided, were followed by periods when she felt in reasonable health. Each 'spasm' seemed to follow a dose of Morley's medicine, but *only* when prepared by the otherwise dutiful Dove. For example, a dose prepared by Mrs Witham brought no signs of trouble.

Amelia Dyer – *Britain's Worst Serial Killer*

Presumed *1860–1896 – Multiple Infanticide; Homicidal Mania/Insanity with Delusions/Melancholia (Unconfirmed), Caversham, Berkshire*
Between March and April 1896, seven infant bodies were dragged from the Thames, alongside the Clappers and Caversham Bridge. All had been strangled and all were attributed to Amelia Dyer. Over the best part of four *decades*, the dreadful 'maker of angels' disposed of literally *hundreds* of babies ... but were her motives purely financial?

Floating Evidence
On **30 March 1896**, the body of a child – Helena Fry – was pulled from the reeds near Caversham Bridge. Barely 1-year-old, she had been cruelly strangled, white tape round her neck and tied in a knot. But it was the brown sheet of paper – wrapped tight round the corpse – that interested Anderson of the Borough Police. For hidden in the creases was a name and address. Nothing prepared him for what was about to unfold.

The address on the parcel led Anderson, a new breed of detective, to an ordinary house in an ordinary street. The terrified occupants knew nought of the matter – not the baby, nor the wrapper, nor the tape or the name. They *did* know a tenant – one Amelia Dyer – who had moved up to Reading a few months before. Anderson quickly discovered her current address.

* * *

On **31 March** Dyer, 57, collected a young girl, Doris Marmon, from her natural mother; having travelled to Cheltenham, where the child had been born. Before heading back, she retrieved a bag made of carpet from the railway cloakroom, and supposedly returned to Reading in Berks.

Instead, she took the baby to an address in Harlesden, north London, where her daughter and son-in-law* were sharing some rooms. During the course of the night, *after the child went 'missing'*, Dyer somehow explained she had handed it on.

The next morning, **1 April**, Amelia and Mary, her daughter, went to Paddington Station, where they met Mrs Sargeant and Harry Simmonds, a

---

*   Mary and Arthur Palmer.

boy. Following a fiscal exchange, they took Harry to Harlesden, with the notion of passing him on.

By the following day, the **2 April**, the baby still 'slept' (he had never awoken!), wrapped up in a shawl that covered his face. Soon after lunch, he had gone, and Dyer explained she had found him a home.

Later that evening, she got a train back to Reading, her bag made of carpet now fastened with string … inside were two bricks and the bodies of two babies … Amelia Dyer had done it again.

* * *

A Grand Piece of Detection

Anderson continued his nascent inquiry, he kept Dyer's house in Reading under continuous watch. He also instructed a colleague to pose as a client – presenting herself as a mother in need.

On **4 April**, Dyer opened the door to receive her new acquisition, but instead Anderson and James* made a dramatic arrest. As they entered the house, the stench of decomposition was later reported as too much to bear.

The search soon revealed two pivotal insights, the clues that enabled the case to unfold. More clothes and apparel than one baby could manage, and pawnbrokers' tickets for so many more.

Fearing the worst, Anderson said the Thames needed 'dragging'.

By **6 April**, Anderson learned of the building in Harlesden, where he discovered more clothing and tickets for pawn. What's more, there was tape, of the type tied round the victims, and he reached the conclusion all three were involved … Arthur Palmer was arrested as 'an accessory *after* the murder'; Mary, the same, but in her case *before*.

On **10 April**, down by The Clappers and Caversham Weir, one of the searchers noticed something submerged. Hauling the carpet bag from the water, Henry Smithwaite peeled open the brown paper wrapping, and recoiled in horror at the sight that he saw. Working with James, they recovered two house-bricks – *and the decomposed bodies of a girl and a boy*.

---

* Sergeant Harry James of Reading Borough Police.

Patterns and Parents

The search at Kensington Road had uncovered a number of letters, which Anderson now used to establish a thread. The two in the river were the pair slaughtered in Harlesden, and two of the letters each bore a name and address. Organising local police to pay the parents a visit, each now identified their child from the bag. With crushing remorse and realisation, both picked out Dyer as the monster they paid.

The horrors of Dyer had begun to unravel; Anderson made contact with the Bristol police. Through some impressive detection, he learned of a couple, who had engaged Amelia Dyer some years before.

In 1891, after handing over their baby, they quickly experienced a complete change of heart. When Dyer was approached, she said the child was no longer with her; and as hard as they tried, she would not tell them why. Some two years later, still plagued by their sorrow, the couple returned, this time with police. That same afternoon, Dyer leapt in the water at Cumberland Basin, in what was considered a (failed) suicide bid.

Multiple Murders ... Multiple Trials

Several coroners' inquests were held throughout April, as more bodies were dragged from the river and their identities learned.* The first, held in great haste on the evening of 11 April, featured Simmonds and Marmon ... and Helena Fry.

After repeated adjournments, the jury declared on the latter: 'wilful murder by person or persons unknown'. Though they hastily added, with an uncertain conviction, that Dyer had *probably* disposed of her rotting remains.

Their findings were clearer with Simmonds and Marmon: the evidence captured left little doubt. Amelia Dyer was indicted for murder; the woman in prison had slaughtered them both.

At the magistrates hearings, they too experienced adjournments – as the number of bodies continued to rise. At its *fifth* reconvening, on 2 May , events took an unexpected and alarming new turn.

Mr Lawrence, Prosecution counsel, admitted not having enough to hold Arthur Palmer; the man was allowed to stand down from the court. In time Mary, too, was released, with no more than a caution. With both gone, it meant Dyer was left on her own.

As though aware of her futile chances, she penned two letters from prison, and handed them over to the matron in charge. She sent them up to the governor's office and their contents were noted as a confession of sorts.

The Bench held its breath while the words were read out.

In the first, she dismissed any notion of Arthur's involvement – no-one but she had known of the crimes. The second amounted to a fuller admission, though it had been intended for her same son-in-law:

> 'To Arthur E. Palmer, Thursday, April 16, 1896. My Poor Dear Arthur,— Oh, how my heart aches for you and my dear Polly! I am send—this to tell you I have eased my mind, and made a full statement. I have told them the truth, that as God Almighty is my Judge, I dare not go into His presence with a lie. You will have a lawyer, but for myself it would only be throwing away money. I know I have done this dreadful crime, and I know I alone shall answer for it. I have just written a long letter, another to mother; also I have wrote out a true and faithful statement of everything. I hope God will give you strength to bear this awful trial.—Your broken-hearted mother, E. DYER' (transcribed from *Old Bailey Proceedings Online*).

Central Criminal Court, 20–22 May

Knowing it only needed one capital sentence, Lawrence proceeded on just the one crime. After staying some time in Holloway prison, Dyer was charged with the murder of the girl in the bag [Doris Marmon]. Her Old Bailey trial should have been a straightforward matter but, unlike the magistrates, another angle arose. Mr Kapadia – Dyer's struggling counsel – decided to enter an insanity plea.

(In)credible Witness

An early witness, William Povey, had seen Dyer carrying a small, brown paper parcel as they passed on the walkway alongside the Thames. It occurred on the morning of the first gruesome discovery – young Helena Fry, who had been caught in the reeds.

On 2 April, John Toller had recognised Dyer as she walked near The Rising Sun pub. She had come up from the river, of that he was certain [which meant she had gone there direct from the train].

Another witness, Jane 'Granny' Smith, had known Dyer since early last summer, and the pair had shared lodgings from then until now. In the days leading up to the raid, there had been a sickening odour, and she had implored Mrs Dyer to take her parcel outside.ʲ

Ironically, the most damning evidence of all came from Mary, Dyer's daughter, repeating the statement she gave Anderson before.

Giving vivid accounts of her mother's behaviour, she painted a picture of madness since being a child.

Mad, Bad – or just Plain Greedy

As the evidence mounted, there was no point in denial – her earlier letters had long seen to that. Expecting the sentence would see her sent to the gallows, Kapadia entered an insanity plea…

Mary claimed that, in 1894, Dyer had threatened to kill her; yet it remained her suicidal desires that drew greatest alarm. On three separate occasions, the young woman reported, her mother had tried to cut her own throat.

Then she confirmed three asylum admissions, two spent in Gloucester, one in nearby Wells. Each was followed by bouts of manic depression, invariably succeeded by violent attacks.

Kapadia's first medical witness, Frederick Logan, related one such admission.

On Christmas Eve 1893, he had arrived at a Bristol address when Dyer attacked him with a poker, insisting he had come to send her away. Using his superior strength to wrench the poker to safety, he deduced she suffered *delusions* with violent affray.

He now recalled how he never doubted her madness:

> '[S]he said she had heard voices telling her the whole time to destroy herself, that the birds said, "Do it, do it". Her daughter was present; she told me that she [Dyer] had been very violent' (based on *Old Bailey Proceedings Online*).

And confirmed he had her admitted without further delay.

Under cross-examination, he denied anxiety was the cause of her trouble, referring instead to a 'disease of the brain'. He had no knowledge of her run-in with parents, or the police who had recently called at her home.

William Bailey Eden (*sic* – actually, Eadon), a doctor in Bristol, recounted his visit a full year on. Reporting violent *delusions*, he had her quickly admitted for a further three months before she was sent on her way.

The principal witness was the alienist, Winslow, no stranger to controversy when appearing in court. He had examined the woman since being arrested, and supported the efforts to declare her insane.

On 15 May, he diagnosed insanity with *delusions*, but added *melancholia* to her list of complaints. He confirmed there were no signs of 'shamming' when she had spoken of voices, which had repeatedly told her to take her own life.

At his subsequent visit, made just four days later, he heard of her night-time illusions (visions he called them at first). In one, she had seen her long-since dead mother, urging her daughter to join her in death. And her natural son, as though he too had departed, though Winslow had known the man was alive.

Now he incurred (yet again) the judge's displeasure when asked his opinion whether he thought Dyer insane. He considered her 'unsound in her mind' [acceptable to the court] and therefore not a responsible agent [which was not]; His Worship insisted only the jury could say.

Winslow, undeterred, expressed his opinion; especially about the partial state of her mind:

'[T]he transient or recurrent form of insanity is the most formidable of its kind … predisposition to an attack is greater in a recovered lunatic than in one who has been always sane … [I]t depends upon circumstances generally—she would be predisposed to an attack at any time' (*Old Bailey Proceedings Online*).

When questioned over Dyer's 'normal' lucid behaviour, he added:

'I should not have expected signs of excitement, because in melancholia … there are no outward evidences of lunacy' (*ibid*).

Contrary medical opinion now came from George Henry Savage, Lecturer on Mental Diseases and Physician at St Barts [Winslow was a lecturer at nearby Charing Cross]. Dyer, he contested, was *not* mentally deficient, and rejected *homicidal mania* as an unlikely cause:

'[T]here is nothing in the manner these two children [Simmonds and Marmon] met their death to suggest homicidal mania, that I see...' Adding: '[A] person may be violent, without being homicidally maniacal' (*ibid*).

Under cross-examination, from Mr Kapadia, he admitted taking his evidence from others' reports. And conceded that:

'[I]n homicidal mania ... voices would probably urge [one] to murder' (*ibid*).

But when pressed further by the inexorable counsel, he retorted in anger:

'I did not conclude the prisoner was suffering from homicidal mania – or [any] kind of insanity!' (*ibid*).

Dr Scott, Medical Officer at Holloway Prison, declared Amelia Dyer as sane as they come:

'I have discovered nothing that is not consistent with her being sane, beyond her own statements of her constant desire to commit suicide, and her memory of recent events being a total blank' (*ibid*).

Questioned later, he denied ever telling Winslow he thought her insane – indeed, on the contrary, he was sure she had 'shammed'. He confirmed there were no signs of her alleged suicide efforts, and added it made little matter at all:

'[S]uicide may attend insanity, or be committed independently of it' (*ibid*).

The very last witness was James Hobley, Amelia's brother; annoyed with his sister and the shame she had brought. Demanding first anonymity, he denied insanity ever ran in the family, inferring hereditary 'madness' was not there to be found:

'[M]y mother was never insane ... there was never a case of insanity in our family, so far as I have heard our family history' (*ibid*).

Verdict and Conclusion

Summing up, Justice Hawkins told the jury that insanity was proved by only one measure – that it followed the Rules laid down half a century before. Had Amelia Dyer known her acts to be wrong ones? Bad dreams and voices were never enough.

In only five minutes, the jury delivered its verdict: the woman was guilty – the woman should hang. Their wish was fulfilled at Newgate in London – she went to the gallows the following June.

Afterwords

Amelia Dyer is still thought of as Britain's most prolific serial killer. Some commentators today believe she murdered 400 or more babies. Some of her victims she knew for a matter of hours; others survived for a number of days.

One last account comes from a letter, received by Amelia while on remand awaiting her fate. Thought to be written by a 'lady of [high] rank and title', it was franked *Monte Carlo* and anonymously signed. The reference to a plea of exculpatory madness remains to this day very easy to read:

> 'I feel convinced that Mr Kapadia will secure you from the extreme penalty if you will only tell him truthfully all you know about your detention in asylums. You should try and clear your daughter Mary. People here sympathise with you because they believe you have periods of irresponsibility, and if that be so you have committed no crime' (*Lloyd's Weekly*, 17 May 1896).

≠ Anderson eventually counted fifty – and Dyer informed him: 'You'll know all mine by the tape around their necks'.

∫ A baby named Isaacs was found on 23 April, and Smith confirmed it was the bundle in question.

Simon Fraser – *A Sleep-Walk Into Hell*

Tuesday 9–Wednesday 10 April 1878 – Murdered His Son; Somnambulism, Glasgow

At Britain's first recorded somnambulism (sleep-walking) trial, Simon Fraser made a rash promise in exchange for his life ... though not before the jury interrupted the hearing.

> *'For then if he [the violent somnambulist] did not take care to prevent himself from doing harm in his sleep to someone, certainly he should be punished'*
> (Sixteenth century, de Covarrubias in Walker 1968: 166).

Simon Fraser's violent act not only shocked a horrified public, but also bemused those who knew him for the good man he was. 28 years old, with a regular income, as a father and husband he was one of the best. So why, when he picked up his 18-month-old baby, did he smash his head on the wall in the room where they slept? His defence for the horror in the house along Lime Street was that 'when he committed the crime, he was [still fast] asleep' (4 Couper: 70).

Court in a Nightmare

At his trial* on 15 July, the court heard how his most frightening dreams involved attacks by wild animals – though the species of beast were seldom known to the world. On the night of the murder the previous April, he claimed to have seen one enter his room. A 'large white beast', he described, rising up from the floorboards, had moved across to his son as he slept in his cot.

With understandable panic, he leapt on the back of the monster, wrestled it away from the boy and dashed its head on the wall. Only when the body went limp, and he stopped and retreated, was he woken from sleep by his wife's terrified screams. His son, with his skull terribly fractured, lay still on the floor and dead to the world.

A Crime in the Making

An apparently peculiar boy, Fraser had been 'slow to learn' and prone to disruption, never more than at night when terrors ruined his sleep. Rising

---

* High Court of Justiciary, Glasgow.

from bed and seemingly conscious, his eyes bore the look of somebody mad. All too often, these unusual somnambulist's wanderings were accompanied by a predisposition for violent assault.

> His beloved sister, Elspeth, became his earliest 'victim', his hands so tight round her neck he left marks on her skin. On another occasion, when still only a child, he threw a punch at his father before he woke up.
>
> Now married, he dragged his wife from their bed and on to the floor; afterwards saying he had dreamt she was caught in a terrible fire and he had pulled her to safety through the perishing flames.
>
> Other examples were not always so harmful – at least for the 'victims' caught up in his dreams. On numerous occasions, he would walk while he slept to a nearby farmyard, while carrying a pitcher as though going for milk.
>
> While living in Norway, he entered a river, to 'save' his sister from 'drowning', though she was tucked up in bed.
>
> And often walked to his work to stack logs in the woodshed [his regular duty], in the dead of the night and still sound asleep.

In all these examples, and innumerable others, people who saw him had sworn him awake. And ever since childhood, with an increasing violence, he had played out his nightmares unaware of his acts.

Or was he…?

A Surprise Interruption

So many and so varied were his eccentric examples, that the jury demanded the hearing be stopped. The foreman confirmed they were all in agreement – they found Fraser *not guilty* for what he had done.

Presiding judge, Lord Justice Clerk, (James Lord Moncreiff) felt the trial should continue. It was only right the trial finished before they proclaimed (cf Westron, *Part 5*). He was keen to hear experts and their considered opinions; in particular, what the gathered alienists said.

An Alienist Assessment

David Yellowlees of Gartnavel Asylum, and Alexander Robertson of the Poorhouse in town, were called by the State as prosecution witnesses, while others were summoned to Fraser's defence. Unusually, both sides concurred in their judgement – though there was still room for manoeuvre in what should be done.

Yellowlees confirmed his belief that the accused – in Scotland, 'the pannel' – had extraordinarily suffered in his sleepwalking states. He conjectured this was due to abnormal blood circulation; which must have occurred in a part of his brain. By its very nature, he continued, a delusion was present: the man must be treated as partially [temporarily] insane.

Robertson agreed – at least that Fraser was guiltless – but he went even further in blaming the mind. Fraser, he said, had a *new* form of condition: which he dubbed '*somnomania*' to the disbelief of the court.

The condition, he explained, made Fraser 'highly excited' as well as 'violent ... [and] dangerous' while 'unconsciousness' of crime. Adding that somnambulism, in fact, was a third state of the conscious, different to sleeping but not awake (4 Couper: 74).

However, he conceded – confusing proceedings – this was no form of madness accepted in law.

With such support from these prosecution witnesses, there was barely the need for the others to speak. Nonetheless, Dr Clouston, of the Royal Asylum, gave his opinion and unsettled the mood. He declared the defendant was sane.

He said there were plenty of sleepwalkers who posed no threat to the waking, the difference in this case was the hideous outcome. He did agree though, that Fraser should escape the rigours of justice, but be sent to a madhouse and not simply set free.*

A Judgement on Murder
Having resisted the jury in bringing an end to proceedings, the Lord Justice Clerk tried to make sense of the views. All too quickly, he summed up his own layman's assumptions: that their verdict remained unchanged after what they had heard.

He directed their verdict in the following terms:

---

* Other so-called mind experts later held the view that Fraser suffered 'violent epilepsy', and that in all probability he was actually awake.

(1) that the jury disregard whether or not sleepwalking was linked to insanity, as it appeared *even the medical profession had yet to agree*; and

(2) to find Simon Fraser *had* 'murdered' his son, but that he 'was in a state…[of] unconscious' and, as such, must have been unaware of his deed. In the cause of the death, 'he was not [a] responsible [agent]' (*ibid*: 75).

In minutes the jury did as instructed.

Medico-Legal Confusion

The unusual verdict brought only bemusement – unusually in both the medicine and law. The man was 'acquitted' of a hideous murder, though nobody declared he be considered insane. In response, the Solicitor General requested a two-day adjournment while the conundrum was measured and opinions were sought. He added how sorry he was to confine Fraser in prison, that it would all be resolved within forty-eight hours (*ibid*).

On 17 July, the hearing continued. A solution of sorts would be thrashed out in court. First, that Fraser spend time at Gartnavel Asylum, doubtless being studied by Yellowlees himself. And second, he should only sleep in his own isolation – and that he committed to do so for the rest of his days.

The Lord Justice Clerk reflected the irregular outcome:

'In respect the Counsel for the Crown does not move for sentence, and in respect the panel *(sic)* has come under certain obligations satisfactory to Crown Counsel [ie to sleep on his own], the Court *deserted the diet simpliciter* (had no intention of further proceedings) against the panel *(sic)*, and dismissed him from the Bar' (*ibid*: 76).

A solution of sorts, but not to everyone's ken.

Had Fraser been acquitted? No, the jury believed he had committed the murder. Guilty? Not really, or he would have been hanged. Insane then? Again, no, his acceptance of time in Gartnavel Asylum did not constitute confinement as a lunatic might.

Instead, they had reached a new, 'special verdict', though no such option existed in the annals of law [in Scotland; unlike its English relation (see Hadfield, *Part 3*)].

Daniel Hack Tuke, the alienist, was especially outspoken, thinking the verdict made a mockery of the alienist cause. He also thought the verdict should have reflected an illness – the epileptic condition the court had ignored.

Fraser's family, it seemed – going back generations – had suffered fits and convulsions, some leading to death (Tuke 1884: 13–16). And *this*, he bemoaned, revealed nocturnal epilepsy; steps should have been taken against further attacks. Condemning Simon Fraser 'as dangerous as a madman' (*ibid*: 16), he never suggested what those steps might have been!

Mary Gallop – *A Gallop to the Gallows*

Saturday 2–Sunday 3 November 1844 – Parricide; Hereditary Insanity, Crewe

In a heart-wrenching case, Mary Gallop knew little but sorrow. But then, had her life been predestined for suffering loss? Her mother, her love and finally her reason – perhaps, in the end, of existence itself. Faced with accusations of lust and an obdurate father, the hapless young girl took her chances with life.

The Wrong Side of the Tracks

When Mary Gallop's mother sliced her own throat – with only Mary as witness – old suspicions of madness came woefully true. For this family from Crewe, it was just the beginning…

Richard, Mary's father, had moved his family from Liverpool, after finding new work in the railway town. Business was booming, with the steam-age expansion, and Gallop senior chanced his arm on locating a job. With his role in the coachworks, and young Mary turned 20, life was passingly good; aside from his loss.

Everything changed when he voiced his concerns over his grief-stricken daughter: '[She is] going like her mother', was all he could say.

All Points to a Tragedy

The imminent, appalling events had their trigger in carnal frustrations; the troubled young woman was desperate for love. A Liverpool lad, her 'boy from the city', was a suitor her father expressly forbade.

In desperation, Mary came up with an answer.

She had only recently heard of the effects of a poison, and a woman who used arsenic for nefarious means. Within hours, she had purchased a clandestine packet, inventing a story of troublesome rats. Fearing the outcome, she returned to the chemist; a second amount was surely enough.

The tragedy unfolded as she prepared tea for the family – her father, two lodgers, four persons in all. Mixing the poison with flour, she made up a meal, and sat back with interest to see how it worked.

The first tragedy came when her father declared he had no hunger for dinner; though the others ate cakes and fell dangerously ill. Surviving the scare, and knowing how much was required, she mixed a third packet with arrowroot, which her father consumed.

Richard Gallop fell ill within minutes of eating, dying later that evening to the family's distress. Mary, though, encountered his passing with scarcely contained and unsavoury glee.

Shunted to Trial

The post-mortem revealed the presence of poison: a word to the police and Mary was lost. In the space of twenty-four hours, she waved goodbye to her father, her lover, her freedom and perhaps even her life.

As news spread of the killing, people leapt to conclusions – had Mary in fact caused her late mother's death? Had she not been alone when that tragedy happened, just as she had been when her father had died? Considered guilty of murder, without even a trial, her neighbours were asking: had she somehow killed two?

Mary was taken to the castle in Chester, where the gaol for the county was but a stone's throw from court.

On 2 December, she faced the Winter Assizes, convinced no-one would care if she were sentenced to death. The appointment of Baron Gurney as Justice – hardly known for compassion – only compounded her sorrow, and with it her luck.

With no family to fight for her uncertain future, Nathaniel Worsdell spoke up for her life. Richard's manager at work had known Mary since childhood, and it seemed he suspected a troublesome mind.

Though often articulate, inoffensive and mild, she could be sullen and morbid, when conditions were right. Alfred Dymond, campaigner for an end to capital punishment, asserted later this proved her champion right:

> 'such … as is indicative of latent insanity which first develops itself in some overt act of mischief or [inexplicable] violence' (1865: 136).

So, too, he continued, an hereditary illness – her mother's mental demise had clearly shown that [notwithstanding the rumours above]. Nonetheless, under Gurney's blatant direction, a guilty verdict was reached – as was her sentence of death.

A Long Line of Complaints

By now, the whole country was watching: a parochial problem was a nation's disgrace. Outrage took hold, as did outcries for mercy, and even the clergy felt driven to act.

Led by Raikes, the Bishop of Chester, they petitioned for clemency in light of the facts. While others set down their own style of pleadings – Worsdell travelled to London to secure her reprieve.

All came to nothing, the death knell pealed loudly. As the Home Secretary, Sir James Graham, repelled a heart-broken Raikes. His cursory rejection, that the case deserved mercy, was met with contempt in the national press (see *Punch*'s 'Justice in Granite', in Dymond 1865: 135).

Timetabled Confession

The press printed Mary's alleged written confession, supposedly narrated and regarded as true. Mr Rowe, Dissenting Minister who remained at her bedside, took plaudits for helping her in 'get[ting] it up'.

When later hounded by those who had fought for her pardon, he was forced to admit things were not as they seemed. He had, he revealed, made up the epistle – taking 'yes' or 'no' answers to the questions he asked! The following is sufficient for setting the tone:

'I shall be twenty-one years of age on the 2nd of next March…Both my father and mother were Wesleyan methodists *(sic)*. My father was a very pious, good man … I recollect him taking me to a Sunday-school *(sic)*,… when I could just walk … I went to the Sunday school belonging to the Brunswick chapel [in Liverpool]. My father afterwards removed to Mansfield-street *(sic)*, and sent me to a Sunday and day school … About ten months after we went to live at Crewe my mother destroyed herself in a fit of insanity… [My father] said he would never give his consent for me to have anything to do with the young man in Liverpool … I thought I should be at liberty [by poisoning her father] to go where I pleased and do as I pleased' (*Lloyd's Weekly* 29 December 1844).

Last Station Stop.

Condemned prisoners in Chester were led from the castle, to the small city prison with its contraption of death. Yet so loud had remained her supporters' vociferous clamour, the authorities chose to move her in the dead of the night.

Their efforts were wasted, the crowd numbered 'thousands'. Mr Hill, police superintendent, was tasked with bringing her out. Arriving just after midnight, on 28 December, she clung to the matron with fear in her heart.

A thick veil was draped over her head and shoulders, she was led to the cart that was standing outside. With the minister, Rowe, and a heavy police escort [many on foot], she made the pitiful journey through the clamouring noise [other reports said the streets were deserted].

Catching sight of the gibbet, her resolve faded to nothing, her legs refusing to function once they had come to a halt. Hill lifted her up and carried her forward, and thus she entered the prison in her 'guardian's' arms.

With just hours to her end, she calmed enough to take coffee, before she was led to the chapel to nurture her soul. [She may have known, had she committed her crime forty years earlier, she would have been taken to Northgate, the old city gaol. The only route to *its* chapel was the walk known macabrely as the town's 'Bridge of Sighs'].

The gaol governor's wife, and their own prison matron, did what they could to lessen her pain. At the last, when the hangman arrived and started to pinion, she found her terror-wracked body refused to comply. Tragic Mary, still seated, was again carried outside.

Dressed in black with a plaid black-and-white shawl, she eyed the thousands who gathered below. While spiritual guides and the intoning clergy all wished her well and prayed for her soul.

Securing her pardon, the hangman shook her hand with great sorrow, and quickly withdrew to the side of the trap. As she sat in her chair, the rope adjusted and tightened, he pulled back the bolt and watched her plunge through the hole...

And that should have been that ... but for her sitting position. Strangulation took several minutes to do what a snapped neck would have done in a blink of the eye. Painfully, slowly, her legs ceased to tremble. Her countenance fell and her body slumped still.

At length, there was only terrible silence. The plea of insanity had lost another to death.

Destined to Fail

Though contemporary dissatisfaction with the hanging of women had already started, any chance of escape was seemingly scarce. First, she was – so-say – a responsible adult; second, she had used poison (which showed deadly intent). Finally, she stood to gain [love] from the death of her father (Smith 1981a: 150). And with no 'obvious' madness, she was doomed to the end.

Those who had taken an interest however, were livid her mind was never considered in court. Gurney, they said, fulfilling his fierce reputation, denied the jury the option she may not have been sane.

Her inevitable destruction was then further cemented by the harshest Home Secretary rejecting their pleas. As Dymond would write, some twenty years later: '[she faced] the most merciless of Home Secretaries, backed by the sternest of *modern* judges' the country had seen (1865: 138, my *emphasis*).

Louis Henry Goule – *Arresting your Demons*

Tuesday 10 June 1845 – Murder [Manslaughter?]; Homicidal Mania (with jealousy), Durham

Accepting that jealousy is a destructive emotion, when worsened by madness it can lead a person to kill. At least Henry Goule, Durham police superintendent, pinned his hopes on that line of defence. For, as Alfred Swaine Taylor wrote four decades later, 'homicidal mania with jealousy' could yet save a man from the rope (1865: [1106]).

[Much of what follows, especially the speech, is taken from the *Newcastle Courant*, 20 June 1845 and *The Times* 31 July 1845 (*19th Century British Newspapers* online)]

The Crime

Some time before 9pm on 10 June, Henry Goule and his wife Emma sat down to their tea. They were late, having returned from a walk by the river; the mood hung heavy with an air of distrust.

Mary Giles – live-in servant and Emma's relation – joined the pair as they picked over unwanted food. Before long, yet again, the talk turned to one issue: Goule's jealous obsession with the men his wife knew.

'Do you think Emma innocent, Mary?' he asked the unfortunate woman.

'I do, I believe that your wife is virtuous, [yes].'

Goule sensed she was being a duplicitous ally: 'Will you swear that?'

'I will.' Mary said flatly. She had always been one for speaking her mind.

Unconvinced, he asked the same questions of Emma, a woman more outspoken than even Mary had been.

'I have been a good wife to you, Henry!'

'Will you swear that you are innocent?' His voice sounded desperate.

No doubt tired of suspicion, her answer was keen: '[No,] I will not!'

Gould was hurt, but Emma continued:

'If you will take my word, I will never deceive you. But you wound my pride by suspecting me.'

Getting up from his seat, he buttoned his jacket and effected a motion as though intending to leave. He then sat back down, but twice more repeated the movement. All the while he had mumbled he needed to go.

Now incensed, she was clearly not finished: 'I will not live with you any longer, as you suspect my virtue!'

The green-eyed monster started to prowl.

Sensing things turning sour, Mary made a suggestion. Perhaps Henry 'should allow Emma to go home to her friends ... [at least until *he* 'got better'].

There, was he not always the one made to suffer? 'I cannot spare her.'

Then he made a proposal all of his own:

'I will go with her!'

Now the tension was building. Mary thought 'both ... were in danger', meaning herself and her mistress, if not Henry himself. Perhaps directed by chance, Emma gazed out the window. Jepson, the surgeon, was wandering by. But it was the man he was with – a fellow named Scruton – the one Henry accused her of meeting in town.

Emma leapt to her feet. 'There [he is]! I will call him.'

'Don't, Emma.' Henry was pleading.

'I will,' she defied him. 'I will call them [both] in, and have this cleared up!'

Goule got to his feet. 'You shall not!'

'I am firm, Henry; you know me.'

And they both entered the hallway, Mary coming behind.

As Emma reached for the door, his hand entered his pocket. Pulling out a pistol, he aimed it straight at her head. 'If you will, then take that!'

As the weapon exploded, she lifted her arm in protection. The ball entered her forearm, shredding the flesh.* 'Oh God!' She threw the door open. 'Murder!'

The two men outside spun round to see the commotion, as she ran on the street, Goule closing behind. He fired again, the shot missing by inches, before she made the house opposite and cowered inside.

Goule now raced toward Scruton, his running like thunder, as the man turned on his heels and fled for his life. Leaping onto his back, Goule sent them both sprawling. Scruton wrenched himself free and scampered away. [Goule was later said to have looked 'like a wild man'.]

---

* The physician, Green, said later the wound was so great he used his finger to locate the 'bullet'.

Thomas Medcalfe, a butcher, alarmed by the racket, tried to set upon Henry but with little success. Thomas Sewell, another – and far more determined bystander – tackled the man in a headlock and pulled the gun from his grasp.

Others came to help, but the chase was concluded, as Medcalfe and Sewell led the 'madman' away. What mattered now was Emma's condition; were her injuries grievous or no more than a graze?

Ebbing Away to a Coroner's Inquest

Though her chance of survival looked better than hopeful, almost a week to the day, things took a turn for the worse. William Green, the physician, had attended the lesion, but fearing infection, his worries came true.

On 16 June, he advised Mary to call in the clergy; the tetanus was raging, lock-jaw would soon come. And, later that evening, despite last minute efforts, poor Emma Goule passed slowly away.

The Coroner's Inquest was convened at the Rose and Crown tavern, but due to the heat they were forced to adjourn. The Grand Jury Room of the (new) prison in Durham was unusually fitting, with Goule on remand in the cells underneath. (Where he had already 'tried' suicide with the blade of a penknife, drawn weakly across the vein in his throat.)

All too soon, the proceedings descended in chaos. When arrested, Goule's notebook had been taken away. He had said at the time, it would shed light on his feelings; the coroner wanted to read what it said.

George Smith, Goule's solicitor, had passed it to Sewell, who had handed it over to the magistrate's clerk. He, having sealed it as evidence for the magistrate's hearing, felt he had to resist it being opened today. In the ensuing debate, at last a solution was offered … Goule himself gave permission when approached in his cell. The book was opened and studied for true revelations, but the coroner dismissed it as shedding no light.

Events Leading To The Assault

The evidence on 24 July at the Durham Assizes was so convoluted that much of it should be kept in the witnesses' own words. The sad circumstances leading up to the injurious moment were outlined to the jury to set the tone for that day…

Mixed with speculation and conjecture, the trail to Goule's murder began twelve months before; when Goule suffered a serious blow to his head while policing a pit strike. Over the following months, he underwent a change in behaviour: his mood became violent with a sense of dismay. His jealousy too grew more desperate and frequent – a view confirmed by Giles, the servant, who had answered his claims:

'I would take my Bible oath of it [she were not unfaithful],' she had told him, but he was not to be sure she was telling the truth.

And when Emma herself turned to Mary for succour, 'she had made up her mind never to live [there] again'. Indeed, she recalled Emma's curious confession: '"If [my] arm was cut open, [I] should get ease, but [I] should never get ease [until] then"'.

The most fearful sign of the impending disaster came with his jealousy, and how it affected his mind: '[His] feeling sometimes drove him almost to madness', she recounted, while he begged Emma not to leave him. And had implored her not to sleep, for fear of his 'thoughts'.

As his envy exploded, he accused her of being with Scruton, though in truth he was the last on a long list of men: 'He did not assign any particular reason for suspecting [Mr Scruton]. He has [often] been jealous of other gentlemen before. In fact, [such] things *had* been getting worse.'

When pressed for details, she reluctantly added: 'He has been very much worse during the last fortnight and has frequently said '"Oh my head, Emma; do not talk to me; my head!"'

Just a fortnight before the fatal shooting, she said he had fainted and seemed not like himself. '[O]n this occasion,' she continued, 'he was quite insensible' – but it was tame to his mood before the tragic event.

She had gone down from her bedroom to find him 'greatly excited … danc[ing] round the kitchen … as if he was [going] insane'. And added, as if to strengthen the picture: 'his hair [was put] up in a wild manner' which he subsequently blamed on the '"pressure of [work]"'.

At 2am on the day of the shooting, Goule's medical attendant, Dr Stoker, had found him in bed. Being 'very exhausted', he gave him some 'restoratives', and ordered plenty of rest. Between 8am and 10am, he visited again, finding him very much improved, though now terribly 'excited'. Goule implored him to have a direct word with his wife; instruct her to 'behave kind to him … not only in word but [also in] deed'.

At 6pm that evening, Goule rose form his bed and paid a visit to Booth – a gunsmith in town he knew reasonably well:

'Booth, I once thought of treating myself with a pair of pistols, but perhaps you will lend me a pair.'

And continued:

'I have to be out tonight to look after some smuggling – some tobacco or spirit that is to be conveyed to Durham – I may be wanted.'

As police superintendent, he often accompanied the Excisemen protecting the county; being armed had become a matter of course. Indeed, Major Wemyss [Durham's first Chief Constable] confirmed Goule told him he was due out that evening, and Booth further revealed he had borrowed pistols before.

An Outcome

At the coroner's inquest, the jury had been told they might bring in a verdict of either murder or manslaughter (or, if they preferred, then neither at all). If they believed Goule got the pistols with premeditated intention – ie of shooting poor Emma – the outcome was murder, of that he was sure. If, however, they thought he fired in a passion, then manslaughter would be the appropriate charge. Everything hinged on why he had borrowed the weapons; his weak state of mind may then come to the fore (paraphrased from the *Newcastle Courant*, 20 June 1845).

The jury took its time in reaching its verdict. In the end, they agreed with the manslaughter charge. Moreover, that 'Emma Goule came to her death by a pistol shot, fired by Louis Henry Goule, *whilst in a state of great mental excitement* on the 10 June 1845' (*ibid*, my *emphasis*).

Now under pressure from the anti-insanity justice, Baron Rolfe's jury considered the facts. After several moments, they arrived at the same clear decision – that Goule was not guilty on account of his mind. It proved a popular outcome:

'The verdict was received with clapping of hands from various parts of the court'.

Final Musings

But what was this madness, on which the jury acquitted? Had jealousy caused insanity – or was insanity the cause? Or had insecure jealousy, a destructive emotion, meant no kind of madness should have been considered at all?

Homicidal mania (*see Part 2*) was the most likely of answers – an irresistible impulse taking charge of his will. While his suicide 'attempt' was regarded by many to confirm his condition, beyond reasonable doubt.

Louis Henry Goule – a husband and killer – was restrained till Her Majesty's Pleasure be known. Emma, his wife, whether true or unfaithful, was laid in her grave for far longer than that.

Moses Hatto – *'A most barbarous murder'*

Tuesday 1 November 1853 – Murder; Homicidal Mania, Burnham, Buckinghamshire

Moses Hatto was condemned by the law for undeniable cunning, yet 'excused' by supporters for his weakness of mind. 'Provoked' into murder, should he have gained control of his torment; or had an *irresistible impulse* proved too much to bear?

Moses Hatto, 23, brought a smile to the eyes of everybody who knew him. Likeable, conscientious, a friend you could trust. Mary Sturgeon however – like him, a servant at Goodwin's Abbey Farm in the county – would go to her grave contradicting that view. Hatto and she had a history of trouble – though most of the household blamed her for their fights. Never mind, she could use him – and his unnatural kindness – the man was a weakling, she was stronger than him…

On Hallowe'en night, leading up to the murder, she asked him for the loan of a sovereign till the end of the week. Hatto refused – she had asked him too often – and it was rare if he ever saw his money again.

Her reaction was savage; she 'twitted' him greatly. He knew how it worked; they had been here before. His rebuff, as she saw it, was going to be punished, and revenge was a dish that was better served cold.

Next morning, 1 November, he pre-empted the troubles, and offered to lend her as much as a crown. Now though, the scorned woman wanted not even a farthing; she had already turned gossip, and to his demise. Suffering all day, he was aware of the slander, and he followed her quietly when she called on next door. Removing his shoes to avoid being detected, he heard her base 'humour', with him as her clown:

> Bunce [groundsman's wife]: 'I hear he's a very big eater.'
> Sturgeon: 'That he is.'
> Bunce: 'Mrs Finch said he was … 'but that he did not eat much bread!'
> Sturgeon: 'But he eats so much meat!'

Silence a while, then the conversation continued.

Sturgeon: 'I am [still] more of a man.'
Bunce: 'Leave him alone – he's hanging himself every day.'

Hatto was incensed. More than that, he was hurt. Creeping back to the farmhouse, he waited for Sturgeon while he considered his move.

As her duties demanded, Sturgeon returned and called him through to his supper. But now he had no appetite except for revenge. Whether to vex him or not, she gave him half his usual beer allowance, a slight he rejected and which led to more words.

Receiving a look he described as 'something pure evil', he made fists of his hands and felt the strain in his nerves. Fighting the urge to strike her down where she stood, he rushed outside to the farmyard, and drew down great gulps of the sobering air.

Re-entering the house, he felt the fire returning.

The wretched woman was coming in from the pantry as he picked up the lard-beater* and raised it high in the air. Bringing it down on her face, her nose splintered and shattered, a tooth and a hairpin bounced off the floor.

He could have done it again, now that he'd started. But to his absolute horror, she had chosen to fight.

Quickly he feared she was gaining momentum, perhaps she was right: she was more of a man. Yet, as he tried to escape, she ran off at a canter, as she fled for her life and the calm of her room.

The weakness he saw reignited his passion, he rose in an instant and set off in pursuit. Stopping to grab the fireside poker, he caught hold of her arm at the top of the stairs. Pulling her hair, he hauled her into the bedroom. Once. Twice. He failed to keep count. When the poker broke in his hand, the wretch was not breathing; yet her unseeing eyes were mocking him still.

Panic Sets In

His mind started thinking, he had to be cunning; there was so little time until his master [Goodwin] came home. Scouring the house, he lifted several items

---

* Lard-beater – 3′ 6″ long piece of iron, rounded at one end and triangular at the other, typically twice the thickness of a regular poker.

– jewellery, a ring, indeed anything light. If only he could make it look like intruders.

He changed out of his clothes and cut them in pieces; even his boots succumbed to a knife. Creeping outside, relieved at the darkness, he stashed the numberless pieces around the estate. [Over the following days, he would dispose of the lot.]

All was now calm, though he still had a corpse; but in no time at all, he had fashioned a plan. At 11.30pm, uncertain how long it had taken, the sound of a horse signalled Goodwin's return. Running to meet him outside, he took the horse to the stable, where he waited and watched as the old boy went in. He was back within seconds, howling and screaming: a fire was raging in one of the rooms.

Hatto and Bunce [groundsman] grabbed buckets of water. Dashing into the bedroom, they met a hideous sight. The woman lay dead, her body consumed by the fire; her legs were already taken by the strength of the flames. Across her trunk lay an old deal table, smashed into kindling though barely alight. While under her head – the eyes staring upwards – someone had folded a napkin to act as a wick.

As Hatto and the others turned to quenching the fire, Goodwin fought back his sickness to search for the truth. Through the billowing smoke, he saw how the woman had suffered. Whoever had done this had bludgeoned her first.

In the on-going commotion, no-one was certain who called the police.

An Inept Inquisition

John Chearsley, the coroner, soon saw for himself this was no ordinary hearing. The police surgeon had confirmed the woman's fatal attack. But pinning the blame for her murder was going to prove much harder. He brought an adjournment while the police went back to the scene.

For unclear reasons, Symington, the police superintendent, looked closer at Hatto than anyone else. On the scantest of evidence, he had him arrested – burns to his hands and blood on his clothes (see Taylor, below). Though he returned to the scene after the coroner's hearing, there was nothing substantial that linked the man to the crime.

When the inquest re-sat on 8 November, Symington had little in the way of new leads. But it was not to get in the way of the jury's 'conviction': a True Bill* was raised to Hatto's dismay.

A Hounding in Bucks
A man sent for trial without proof of involvement[1] had come to the ears of the Metropolitan Police. Despatching one of their best [Langley], Scotland Yard took the lead in unravelling the truth.

And whether by chance or clever detection, it brought a breakthrough of sorts (though still not enough).

The fire, it seemed, could not have been started by the one in the grate – it had never been lit! It removed one niggling doubt – that it had been accidental; it had been set by the killer to conceal the death.

Hatto's burns now grew in evidential importance – especially when naphtha was shown as their cause. The flammable oil was known for making fires a furnace – a favourite aid when burning on farms.

An 'Outrageous' Result
The trial began later that winter. Circumstantial evidence was accepted as proof. Found guilty of murder, he was handed his sentence; it was now his supporters who must garner the truth.

Reaction outside descended into civil disruption; especially when Lord Campbell, the judge, was so quick to condemn:

'I entertain no doubt of your guilt. A murder, one of the most barbarous recorded in the annals of the country has been committed, and you must forfeit your life for it. You must expect no mercy in this world, but prepare for another. I beseech you repent of your crime, and prepare for the awful charge that awaits you' (*Wrexham and Denbigh Weekly Advertiser* Saturday 11 March 1854).

With his life in the balance, efforts were made to save Hatto. But when petitioned for respite, the Home Secretary said:

---

* Cases considered suitable for full trial at the next Assizes.

'Those who meditate murder know that the gallows impends and are deterred. You cannot convince me that punishment of death has not this effect' (Oates 2012: 27).

With echoes of John Howison (*see Part 5*) some two decades earlier, his supporters tried everything to buy him more time. Their one main concern was his mental derangement, which the judge and the jury had simply ignored.

Then Hatto himself pulled the rug from under their efforts ... his chances were ended and so was his life.

A Mad Man's Confession?

On 25 March, the newspapers gleefully printed Moses Hatto's confession – the police, after all, had been right all along. Not only had he now admitted to murder, he also revealed things detectives should be able to prove. [Critically this included where he had hidden his clothing, with detailed descriptions of where he had been before placed on remand.]

Recounting the murder, he gave a telling description – and nobody doubted he was telling the truth. But to those who knew 'better', he was not just confessing; he was writing out his insanity plea:

> 'I was so throwed, that I hardly knew, indeed, I did not know where I was, or what I did. I stood with my hand clenched, ready to strike her; but I could not. Then she went into the larder. I then took the iron lard-beater, and stood at the door, thinking to strike her down as she returned, *but I could not do it, and thinking to drive it out of my mind, I went out of doors.* I wished I might hear my master returning home. Then I went in again. She again went into the lard-house. I again took up the lard-beater, and, on her return, I knocked her down in the passage' (*Morning Post*, 25 March 1854, my *emphasis*).

This personal struggle, to catch hold of *volition*, was now cited as proof of the state of his mind. Hatto had been driven insane *before* he committed the murder – the 'poor man' had suffered a 'loss of control'.

In this, the alienists too saw *homicidal mania* – a condition distrusted each time it was used. Often accompanied, so say, by an *irresistible impulse*, Hatto they insisted deserved to be saved.

Another Verdict Entirely

Time, though, ran out for poor Moses Hatto. On 24 March, Calcraft* arrived in his cell. Pinioning him first, in the usual manner, he led his 'companion' to the gallows outside.[2]

Moments later, he became the first execution since Aylesbury prison had been built in the town. Robert Gibbs, editor of the local *Buckinghamshire Herald*, recorded it all in his account of the times:

> 'Moses Hatto has been executed on the top of the entrance to the new County Gaol at Aylesbury [Bierton Hill]. From the time of his receiving his sentence he conducted himself in a way entirely befitting his position and died with Christian fortitude and resignation' (*Local Occurrences* (1878–82)).

Insane After All?

It has since been left for others to comment on whether the man was insane at the time of his crime. Alfred Swaine Taylor (*see Part 1*) remained comfortable with the jury's decision – though he acknowledged the plea should still have been made. [Never mind that Taylor was consulted as part of the trial.]

He had recently determined his favoured condition – the one Hatto suffered but which was strongly ignored. Like the alienists, he suggested *homicidal mania* – joined by an *irresistible impulse*, he had failed to control.

What would have aided his chances to keep him free from the gallows was if he suffered *delusions* that disrupted his *will*. It was never enough, Taylor accepted, he had known a right from a wrong, as laid down in the Rules.

Then there was Hatto's gallows confession; and what really those few words were worth. As in Howison's case (*see Part 5*), it might yet reveal the confessor's insanity, rather than being a genuine effort at cleansing the mind. [If he had suffered *suicidal mania*, a fictitious confession could yet get him hanged.]

Reading it over, he saw glaring omissions.

Hatto claimed to have pushed Sturgeon's corpse to the fire (grate) – yet the investigation discovered this could not have been true (*see above*). Second, and

---

* William Calcraft, renowned executioner.

maybe even more damning, he 'revealed' to the police where he had hidden his clothes. When these sites were explored, long after his hanging, nothing was found that supported his claims.

Finally, Taylor had held on to his most devilish knowledge, afraid to admit it for a decade or more. His inquiries then had been restricted to clothing; that is, the things Hatto was wearing when Goodwin came home. He accepted now that the bloodstains he found there could have come from helping put out the fire and not from the crime.

Footnotes

1. Other evidence was alleged to prove Hatto's involvement – such as a smearing of blood to a door locked from inside [ie only he and the victim were in the house at the time].

2. The outcry that followed Hatto's *public* execution saw the people of Aylesbury petition the Lords. The Bishop of Oxford, for a long time their champion, demanded capital punishment was best hidden from view. His opponent, Lord Campbell, interrupted the motion – but then he was the judge who condemned Hatto to die. Not until fourteen years later did Aylesbury [and Britain] get what it wanted: no more hanging in public, whatever the crime (*see Appendix 2*).

John Howison – *A Miscarriage of Justice?*

Friday 2 December 1831* – Murder; Partial Insanity, Cramond, Edinburgh
Was the execution – and dissection – of John Howison in Edinburgh a miscarriage
of justice or an unavoidable end? Was he, in fact, sane when he committed a
murder? Or was society not yet receptive to the alienist claims? Ignoring the
chance he may not have committed the horror, was his death another 'inhuman
killing' – the phrase used to describe the original crime?

On 2 December 1831, in the small village of Cramond, the widow Old Martha
Geddes bid farewell to her friends and watched as they hurried back to their
houses; there were reports of a vagrant seen hanging around.

Barely had she returned to her chair and her knitting, when a rap at the door
tripped the beat in her heart. Nobody knocked here, the doors were always left
open – which meant he or she was a stranger. She found she was scared.

Ninety minutes later, when called on by a girl selling seafood, Old Geddes was
found with her head spliced in two. A nearby spade had been used to divide her
face down the middle, while a rough, crooked stick had been left on the floor.

No-one recalled how long the screaming continued.

With news of the vagrant, the authorities swept over Cramond. The man had
been seen going into the house. A lad on the quay saw him leave in a hurry.
Within twenty-four hours, John Howison was found:

> '[A] middle aged man, rather thin, dark complexioned, and about five feet
> nine inches in height. He wore a black hat, a darkish green coat, with
> metal buttons, and a black or dark coloured handkerchief round his
> neck, which came up so as to cover his mouth' (*Caledonian Mercury*, 3
> December 1831).

So great was his violence when they tried to arrest him, they trussed him up like
a sack and dumped him in the back of a cart. And thus he arrived at Edinburgh's
most notorious prison – Calton Gaol, Regent Road – a vision of hell.

---

* Though committed six years before Victoria's accession, the arguments it provoked were
very much of the time.

Insanity Brooding?

Howison, a native of Blackfriars Wynd in the capital city, was believed to be around 44 years old. To their surprise, the authorities learned he had, until recently, been known for his kindness and possessed a sartorial splendour now belied by his rags. In the events leading up to the crime – but discovered only *after* the murder – his character had undergone the most radical change.

In the past, he had quickly grown grubby; his temper morose, his habits unkempt. An uncontrolled glutton, he had a liking for liver – two pounds, eaten raw washed down with the blood. Aside from his food, he engaged in crass superstition: pricking himself with a pin and sucking the wounds. He sprinkled salt on his head, to stop the witches attacking and had a bible on cord, which he strung round his neck.

Completing the image:

'He subsisted by begging, was noted for his religious eccentricities, wore an antique dress, allowed his beard to grow to a prodigious length, and delighted to attend the services of all the dissenting communities in succession' (Dymond 1865: 169).

An Insanity Plea

Those who knew him insisted he was brighter than most, that he knew a right from a wrong, and the error of crime. But, according to others, he suffered frightening *illusions (see Part 2 –* cf *delusions)*, and *a crippling pain in his head* that many blamed for his ways.

Growing aware of his troubles, a local alienist, Dr Combe (see eg bibliography) offered to finance his trial; indeed, he urged the Solicitor-General [Lord Cockburn] to accept the insanity plea. If Cockburn was tempted, it failed to transpire, as the nature of madness was usurped by the Rules (*see Part 3*):

'Very possibly [Howison] did think he was obeying God's command, but he knew he was breaking man's law [eg by fleeing the scene] ... [and] exhibited *a knowledge of having done wrong*' (*ibid*: 170, my *emphasis*).

On New Year's Eve, Howison stood trial at the High Court in the city. Despite Lord Cockburn's reluctance, his mind was assessed. Lord Justice Clerk [David Lord Boyle] went so far as to permit alienist witness – though the defendant himself maintained he was sane.

His recent behaviour was carefully questioned, with evidence given from the home where he lodged. Mrs Crombie, the landlady, had seen the change in his manner, noted unsociable habits and his sinister ways. She also reported how he only liked children and kittens, and shunned adult company to become a recluse.

The young lad from the quay, who gave the police his description, said he had seen Howison running from Widow Geddes' house. While the jury were told of his religious obsessions: that he was a practising Catholic, though he preferred the Quakers[†] these days. He was thought to be fierce in his religious convictions, as though religion itself was more important than creed.

Lodging an insanity plea, the medics failed in their quest to reach an agreement – though they drew the *likely* conclusion he was mad at the time:

> 'it was *probable* he had laboured under some hallucination or mental delusion when he committed the deed' (*ibid*, original *emphasis*).

His implied guilt was not lost on the struggling jury – though Howison maintained he was an innocent man. When pushed on the fact he had been *seen* in the village, even entering and leaving Geddes' house, he made the not unreasonable point, with no fear of rebuttal, that nobody had seen him carry out the attack.

The Verdict

The conclusion was reached that Howison knew that what he had done had been cold-blooded murder. While 'evidence' was given that he had 'concealed the deed'. [Reports failed to state what those efforts had been.] At 3am on New Year's Day, the jury delivered its verdict. The accused was found guilty; his sentence was death.

Before returning to Calton, he was forced to confront an additional horror as Lord Justice Clerk Boyle considered his fate. In an act of brutal contempt, he promised his body to science, for the Edinburgh surgeon, Munro, to dissect. [The last of its kind before the 1832 Act (*see Appendix 1*)]

[†] The Society of Friends insisted they declined his inquiry, *as they thought him deranged in his mind from his peculiar manner* (*EMSJ* 38: 53).

In the following weeks, attempts were made to prove Howison's madness. Yet even a Quakers' appeal to the king brought no gain. A memorial seeking the Home Secretary's Mercy was cruelly and simply referred back to court.

'Confession'

Late on 20 January, he was taken from Calton to the nearby 'lock-up', as was the custom on the night before death. He rejected demands to confess to the murder, but fired up interest in what was left of his life:

> 'No, I will never confess that [the Cramond murder] ... but I will tell you something tomorrow morning that will astonish you [all]!' (*Caledonian Mercury*, 23 January 1832).

At 4am, astounding everyone present, he made a terrifying claim that he had killed many more. They included six children, he said, and men killed in the forest; before he went on to list many besides. Whatever the number, its truth was rejected – the head of police said they were very alive!

From madness or mischief, his eyes rolled around wildly; his body shaking, though he was chained to the wall. 'He was mad enough then,' Dymond lamented, 'but it was too late to appeal' (1865: 171), the hour of his death was almost at hand.

At a little past 8am, he was led to the scaffold [at Lyberton (Libberton's) Wynd], where he was passed a customary white hankie to drop when prepared. Throwing it back in the face of the terrified hangman, he uttered: 'You may give [the signal] yourself [I refuse to give mine]!'

The man stepped away from the prisoner, as the clergy intoned, pulled back the bolt and watched John Howison fall.

Aftermath

Dymond condemned the events: '[H]e was dragged from his cell and hanged, *a raving maniac*' (*ibid*). And the world had to face another difficult test: had Howison been *mad* enough to claim crimes he had never committed, or *bad* enough to feign madness just to escape from the rope? In the end, he had hanged for the want of an answer.

The Scottish advocate, James Simpson – who attended the trial – was moved to confess later his bitter regret. In hindsight, he wrote, Howison had *not* been a responsible agent; and his later dissection only worsened his fate (*Anatomy at Edinburgh* – see bibliography).

What remained suggested a *miscarriage of justice* – a sentence delivered, regardless of truth. 'Evidence' had been at best circumstantial: the man seen leaving Old Geddes' cottage might have been fleeing the scene having found her remains.

An Inalienable End

More worrying still, especially for the future of the insanity mantle, was how the alienists' failure attracted scorn and contempt. The [notoriously unreliable] Broadside Ballad observed drily: 'of course, [among them] there were various opinions' (1832, *F.3.a.13(20)*). While the erstwhile *Spectator* wailed its disdain for their sort: '[t]hey spoke, as medical men in such situations seem destined to speak, so that neither Judge, Jury, nor spectator, could tell what they thought or what they meant' (7 January 1832).

In hindsight, it is back to Dymond wherein lies the possible answer – offering both the motivation for murder [*paranoia*], and the malady claimed:

> 'His chief peculiarity or **monomania** ["morbid delusion"] was a dread of the influence of witches. He had an especial horror of old women who might possess supernatural powers, covering his body with marks, as spells against their influence, and wearing a Bible in his bosom as a further protection' (1865: 169).

Prichard (*see Part 1*), though, preferred his own diagnosis, leaving him to offer a view on the case. Suffering from *moral insanity*, Howison 'fell, a victim to ignorance' (quoted in Lockhart Robertson 1847: 166). Had Howison hanged when he should have been saved?

Roderick Maclean – *'It is worth being shot at – to see how much one is loved!'*

Thursday 2 March 1882 – High Treason; Insanity and Treason, Windsor
Queen Victoria could be forgiven for thinking she was an unpopular monarch. From her accession in 1837 to the end of her reign in 1901, she was shot at (six times), beaten (on the head with a brass-topped cane) and had her apartments invaded by drunkards and 'madmen'.

In March 1882, the case of Roderick Maclean left its own indelible mark – not just on the queen's nerves, but on crime, insanity and her place with her subjects. First, and unlike the others, Maclean's pistol was loaded! Second, it caused Victoria to demand a change in the law. Third, it revealed a monarch quite out of touch with a nation's compassion – at least for handling the criminally insane.

Since 1800
Long before Hadfield's trial at the start of the century (*see Part 3*), crimes against monarchs had shaped the insanity debates. In the aftermath of his hearing, the so-called 'Criminal Lunatics Act' (40 Geo. III, c. 94) was rushed into being, introducing a new 'special verdict', for confining 'the mad'. Without it, Hadfield would have been unjustly hanged or wrongly set free.

Two further points were introduced by the new legislation: both pertinent to Maclean's trial some eighty years on. The accused could be found 'not guilty on the ground of insanity'; and they could now be confined 'until His (Her) Majesty's Pleasure be known'.

Three years after Victoria's accession, further amendment was considered a pivotal need. The special verdict had been set for only serious felons, while less grave misdemeanours were kept from its reach. In 1840, The Insane Prisoners Act [3 & 4 Vict., c. 54] amended the error.

Heralding another rushed piece of new legislation (1842), a young William Bean fired his gun at the Queen. Until then, the post-Hadfield law had made little distinction between capital High Treason and a desire to alarm [Bean's revolver had been packed with harmless tobacco]. The Treason Act [5 & 6 Vict., c. 51] 'for the further Security and Protection of Her Majesty's Person' helped save madmen [like Bean] from a trip to the gallows, while protecting the monarch from the criminally *sane*.

Finally, when Lieutenant Pate (1850) brought his stick down on the magisterial temple, he was found guilty of high misdemeanour and sent abroad for seven years (Smith 1981a: 126). The noteworthy impact was the monarch's frustration – at the piecemeal legislation every time she was harmed.

By the time Maclean took his 'pot-shot', she had suffered enough. Yet her strident response lost her place with the public – on criminal lunatics, she was missing the point.

The Case of Roderick Maclean, 1882

Roderick Edward Maclean, 28, was an 'out-of-work' artist. Sixteen years earlier, he received what his counsel now called a severe bang to the head. In 1874, his parents were issued with a medical certificate, confirming their son was 'not right', at least in his head. Yet it was not until 1880 that action was finally taken, and he was sent to the asylum where he remained for twelve months.

Attack

On 2 March, Victoria arrived into Windsor railway station, where she was met by her carriage for the ride up the hill. In the crowd was Maclean who, in extreme agitation, raised his hand, trained his pistol and fired a shot.

The Queen heard the projectile as it hissed past the carriage, and the commotion that followed as Maclean was dragged to the floor. The public screamed 'Murder!' and shouted out for the monarch, while two boys struck him hard with the brollies they held.

Trial ... for High Treason

Damning proof of intent was recovered the next day, when the bullet was found in a nearby wall. It was clear he had shot 'in a direct line' with the carriage – while a note in his clothing confirmed his design! Thus, he was charged with two separate offences: in effect, his *intent* and his *attempt* to succeed. A rare sitting of the Special Commission (State Trial) was convened on 19 April at Reading's main court.

Silence!

Counsel related what had brought them to trial, while Montagu Williams [Maclean's appointed attorney] sat watching in silence and refused to engage. In truth, he had known there was no earthly merit – the first-hand accounts would be hard to disprove. When he got to his feet, he spoke on only one subject – what mattered now was Maclean's state of mind.

From the off, he proclaimed that no *right-minded* person, would shoot at the monarch unless they were mad. He sought to prove to the jury how Maclean should be pitied; not found guilty of treason and sent to his death:

> 'The prisoner … ought not to be made liable for intentions; he was a person who was not responsible for his actions, and, instead of being the object of loathing and execration, ought rather to be the object of commiseration' (reported in *The Times*, 20 April 1882).

Putting it On?

The first called to the stand was the eminent Maudsley (*see Part 1*), who had issued the certificate when Maclean was a child. He recalled nothing particular about that historical visit, but insisted he must have had evidence to make such a claim. When questioned by counsel if the boy may well have recovered, he accepted the chances could not be denied. But when examined again by Montagu Williams, confirmed it was likely that he had probably not.

More recent examples of the accused's ongoing madness came in the form of a letter, dated two years before [May 1880]. Addressed to his sister, it revealed Maclean's provocation came from the strangest of sources and the queerest of things.

The ranting included his now infamous phrase (in italics):

> 'Dear Annie – I have no doubt but that you will be somewhat surprised to receive another letter from me, but as the English people have continued to annoy me, I thought I would write, as you should not be surprised if anything unpleasant occurred, as the people being so antagonistically inclined towards me, makes me raving mad. I can hardly contain myself in fact. I mean, *if they don't cease wearing blue, I will commit murder*' (*ibid*).

He concluded the missive with the ominous promise:

> 'If I cannot commit a murder … in one way, I will in another' (*ibid*).

And ended:

'[I]f there is [any] more difficulty, there may be more victims' (*ibid*).

Another, dated the next day, shed light on a likely condition – some saw clinical *delusions* in the words that he used:

'I received your telegram this morning, and as the people where I am staying heard me say something about *the revenge I contemplate having against the English people*, as they have all conspired to annoy me – I am not alluding merely to Weston [-super-Mare, his present address], but every one in England, in London, Bristol, Bath, and Boulogne, in fact everywhere – ... I have no doubt it would drive any one mad if they knew for certain, as I do, that millions of people are trying to injure, annoy, and vex me on every opportunity' (*ibid*).

Dr Hitchings, who had seen him around the time of these ravings, confirmed he thought Maclean was troubled by illness of a particular kind. Not just delusions but *homicidal mania* – with no doubt an *irresistible impulse* to kill.

More medics were called – the 'modern' mad-doctors – all of whom met him while held on remand.

Henry Manning of Laverstock Asylum near Salisbury, confirmed Maclean suffered three *homicidal delusions* which he spelled out to court:

(i)   the people of England attempted to starve him;
(ii) their wearing of blue was designed to provoke;
(iii) he had supernatural powers through 4 as a number.

Taken together, he was surely unhinged.

When asked if he thought Maclean knew what he was doing, Manning was quick to confirm that, in his opinion, he did. When asked if he thought Maclean discerned the wrong in his actions, he repeated the answer, then went on to add more. Maclean, he suggested, was *impelled* by delusions: It was '[a]n absolutely irresistible moral impulse, as strong as [any] physical [force]' (*ibid*).

In such high-profile cases, there were so many 'experts', but all now agreed Maclean's mind was deranged. With his history of trouble, it was a foregone conclusion that, at some time or other, he would commit such a crime.

Summing Up

In consequence of the fact that Maclean faced the charge of High Treason, he could be sentenced to hang if a guilty verdict was brought. The Lord Chief Justice, Lord Colcridge, gave a lengthy assessment allowing the jury to work things out in their mind.

Citing cases where pleas of insanity had brought only unbridled confusion, he reminded those present of the law on the Rules (*see Appendix 3*). Their meaning and impact, he tried to assure them, must still be applied even though they were fifty years old.

In actual fact, they soon arrived at their verdict … Maclean was 'not guilty, on the ground of insanity'; the judge said he must be detained till Her Majesty's Pleasure be known.

Much **un***amused*

Victoria's *dis*pleasure was understandably forceful … another acquittal proved too much for the queen. Ahead of the trial, she had contrived to show bearing:

'It is worth being shot at – to see how much one is loved!' (quoted in Walker 1968: 188).

But now that the jury had rejected their duty [to find him guilty], she was rapidly moved to harden her tone.

Just four days later, she demanded a change in the statute:

'[I]f this was the necessary effect of the law, Her Majesty thinks it worth consideration whether the law should not be amended' (*ibid*: 189).

Reeling from scores of attacks, she bestowed her opinion. With scarcely concealed anger, she claimed the law should have done more. Even lunatics, she said, needed exemplary teaching; with gaol or the rope to dissuade them from crime.

Her words brought her rank isolation, amidst claims she was foolish on the topic in hand. Her rhetoric, said the press, suggested poor understanding – of the nature of law if not of the mind. And in particular, they wailed that she ignored someone's loss of *mens rea* [ie legal awareness – *see Part 2*] – and that compassion was something that had passed the queen by!

It may help to explain her unpopular viewpoint, to remember how close she had come to her death. For, unlike the others, Maclean's gun had been loaded – a steadier aim would have meant a new king.

Roderick Maclean spent the rest of his life – almost a full forty years – in Broadmoor Criminal Lunatic Asylum, near Reading in Berks. He died on 8 June 1921 – his case notes are still subject to the hundred years rule. In 1883, a new Act was delivered: The Trial of Lunatics Act (46 & 47 Vict., c. 38) brought in a new term. 'Guilty but Insane' replaced the former 'Not guilty on the ground of insanity', which Victoria moaned was no deterrent to crime.

Hannah Moore – *'She had better speak the truth'*

Saturday 15 November 1851 – Infanticide; Irresistible Impulse, St Leonards, East Sussex

The tragic case of Hannah Moore and her ill-fated baby highlighted numerous aspects of the insanity debates. Attitudes towards women who killed were about to cause mayhem, not just in the verdict but in the sentencing too. Another legal conundrum – admissibility of a killer's confession – added fuel to the fire in these difficult times. Behind it all lay a more innocent victim.

Crime – the First

On Saturday 15 November 1851, Hannah Moore – 23-year-old servant at St Leonards presbytery near Hastings – felt decidedly unwell. Ignoring the pains in her stomach, she carried on with her duties, but at lunchtime relented and took to her bed.

Alone in the house, she fought off despair as she gave birth to her child.

Using a cloth she had brought from the kitchen, she wound a tourniquet tight round the poor infant's throat. Twisting it three or four times, she stifled its cries as she shut off its breathing, then bound the chin with a duster and waited for calm.*

A noise from downstairs announced an unwanted intruder. Hannah called out: 'Mrs Lamb, is that you?' The person below confirmed her suspicion, followed closely by footsteps as she ascended the stairs.

Pushing open the door, Lamb looked in on the bed-stricken woman. 'You look like –'

She paused. A small pool of blood on the floor caught her eye, and the footprints that led to a small box to the side.

'You look,' she repeated, growing aware of a smell. 'Like a person who has had a miscarry.' Her voice was accusing. 'Or a child.'

'Oh dear me,' Hannah replied, 'nothing so bad as that, Mrs Lamb. Thank God!'

[dialogue taken mostly from *Hastings & St Leonards News*,
28 November 1851]

---

* At the Coroner's Inquest and Sussex Assizes, Gardiner confirmed – in graphic, upsetting detail – how the baby appeared – the face black, the tongue protruding.

Crime – the Second

On Wednesday 19, three traumatic days later, Hannah called on the woman but found she was out. In her hands she carried a tightly wrapped parcel. The plan hadn't worked – where *was* Mrs Lamb?

'She's not in,' spoke a neighbour, who had seen Hannah knocking. 'Can I help you at all. I don't know when she's back.'

Hannah spun round. 'May I have use of your privy?'

But for whatever reason, the woman refused. She did, however, lead Hannah to a more public toilet – at the back of the houses in a nearby road. Though technically private, the door was left open; those who had need were never caught short.

Hannah bid her goodbye and shut herself in the closet, wishing more light would break-up the gloom. Untying the parcel, she gazed down on her baby, wrapped up in an apron she had the foresight to use.

Without pausing, she dropped the small bundle, through the hole in the toilet and watched as it sank. Then closing the door, she hurried to safety; the evidence hidden, all traces now gone.

Discovery

Late that same night, a young girl used the same miserable privy, when she saw something white almost submerged in the filth. Racing back to her house, she returned with her grandfather who, in no time at all, used the tongs he had brought.

Lifting up the small bundle, he gasped out in horror – then dropped it again, and it sank in the slime. He had to get help ... he ran off for the policeman ... the girl waited behind ... there was no time to explain ...

Barnes, the nearest on duty, ran to the privy. Lifting the bundle back out, he opened it up. The dead baby inside had been no more than a few hours old.

Detection

On hearing the news, with a little inquiry, Mrs Lamb arrived quickly at the horrible truth.

The next day (Thursday 20), she confronted the girl in the Presbytery kitchen: 'Oh, Hannah, *what* have you been doing?'

She looked back abashed: 'Nothing. Of course.'

'A child has been found.'

Moore looked ready to buckle. 'I hope you will not think it was [in any way] me!'

Now the cook, who had listened to the unusual chatter, thought it time she rebuffed the uneven attack. 'Never mind Hannah, it is not yours,' she exclaimed in an instant.

Mrs Lamb held her tongue; she would leave it. For now.

Some little while later, she approached Gardiner, the surgeon, who had examined the boy at the grandfather's house. As she shared her suspicions, he agreed to see Hannah; a brief consultation would reveal any signs. Indeed, he had seen her on many occasions – and was sure she had been pregnant, if not then how far gone.

In the presence of the cook and her own dear sister, Gardiner examined his patient with particular care. Soon enough, he found evidence of trauma – the girl had given birth, of that he was sure.

Proposed Diagnosis

The Coroner's Inquest took place the following Friday; but early that day, he [Gardiner] returned to the house. Hannah, he learned, had something to tell him; after holding her silence, she now wished to confess. She told him of the pressure from her mistress, Mrs Gordon, that in this, as in all things, 'she had better speak the truth'. It had led her to choose the right course of action – but its coming about would bring questions in court.

In a faltering voice, she revealed how she had murdered the baby, how she secreted his body in a box under her bed. She hid the afterbirth contents in the Presbytery toilet [subsequently found lodged in the trap] and had taken the corpse to where it was found.

During the inquiries that followed, a fellow servant revealed how Hannah had confessed that it had not been her intention [to kill]. But some *irresistible impulse* had taken control of her actions, as though she had lost all inhibition and control of her will.

Trial

In the debates of the mid-nineteenth century, there was growing disquiet at the favourable treatment women were shown. On the insanity plea – of *puerperal madness* – they were escaping with murder as the body count grew.[†] By the time Hannah came to court, she was probably expected, if not to walk free, then to avoid being hanged.

The hearing was delayed on the grounds of an illness, which kept her confined until 18 March. She took her place in the dock at the Sussex Assizes surprised, like the rest, at how it would end.

Though no formal insanity plea had been entered, and with no medical witness [other than Gardiner], the jury itself disputed her mind. Having heard all the evidence, they took three quarters of an hour, to arrive at their verdict – guilty as charged. They added, before the judge could pass sentence, that they recommended her to mercy, as they thought her insane.

Baron Parke – presiding judge, not known for compassion – took issue with the jury and their impertinent views. If, he ordered, they had any thoughts on that subject, they must reconsider their judgement and try the prisoner again.

A further fifty minutes went by, before the foreman repeated: 'Guilty … of the concealment of the birth … *not* guilty of [death]!' Adding: '[We] are not certain of the prisoner being in complete possession of her faculties, [at least] at the time [she disposed of the birth]' (*Hastings & St Leonards News*, 28 November 1851).

Parke's countenance had sunk even further.

Everyone an Expert

The jury, not experts, declared Hannah unstable. At least at the time she committed her crime. The outcry was rabid … not just from distaste for saving inexcusable women. No alienist had proved the 'madness' she bore.

To many, she slaughtered her minutes-old baby for the scandalous reason of keeping her job. Was that not the reason for confessing her actions? The Presbytery mistress had told her she should.

Parke, passing sentence, gave her two years for concealment – *the same sentence he gave for the stealing of sheep*. He could not even send her to the local asylum – after two years' hard labour, she would be out on the streets.

---

† See 'Mad Women, Bad Women' – *Part 4* – for background

'Court for Crown Cases Reserved'

But there was still enough time for one more gasp of amazement. Hannah had come within inches of not standing trial at all. As Parke now revealed, her confession was doubtful. Mrs Gordon, her mistress, had placed her under duress.

At the start of the hearing, he had consulted his colleagues, as to whether Hannah Moore's words could be accepted in court. The consensus was reached – it was a valid confession – her mistress would not form any part of the trial. Moreover the alleged crime had not, so they argued, interfered with her ability of doing her job.*

Parke still reserved both the case and conviction, until the point had been challenged in the national court.** On 14 June, it considered the question; and agreed with the opinions Parke had sought.

After all the close scrutiny, one thing was now clear. Moore's conviction was legal – *such as it was.*

---

*   The question of admissibility was reduced to the fact that Hannah's confession had been wrought by 'a wife'. As her husband was never a prosecution witness, and the crime had no bearing on his wife's running of home, notwithstanding her influence on Hannah as one of their servants, the confession was good and the sentence could stand.

** The Court for Crown Cases Reserved could only challenge points in law – it did not sanction appeals.

Jane Parnell – *Hell Hath No Fury*

Monday 6 January 1851 – Perjury; Faked Insanity (Hysteria), Bethnal Green, Middlesex
An unusual – and, here, 'light-hearted' – case, in which a 25-year-old woman claims the hysteria condition as her means of defence. Four weeks earlier, she accused another of trying to kill her. But then, hell hath no fury like an ex-lover scorned.

Parnell was wronged – at least that's what she argued – having made a career out of stretching the truth. In what appears to have been a jealous act of destruction, she – and her accomplice – staged an imaginary crime.
    [taken from *Old Bailey Proceedings Online*: t18510106-384, t18510203-546]

A Murderous Attack; or Trial – The First
One Edith Hopwood charged with assault and intent to commit murder:

> 'Jane Parnell was assaulted in Ramsay-street [Bethnal Green], on 2 December 1850, between six and seven o' clock in the evening, by a man and woman with masks on, that the woman drew an instrument across her throat, and that Mrs Hopwood was the woman' (*Old Bailey Proceedings Online*).

At the Central Criminal Court, on 6 January 1851, George Hopwood, a backgammon board maker, revealed his ill-fated affair with the woman, Jane Parnell. But the self-proclaimed victim had brought nothing but woe…

Taking a decision he later regretted, Hopwood moved out of his house and moved in with Parnell. All too soon he discovered he had acquired a problem – the devious woman was married as well! The rows that followed landed Hopwood in prison – though the charge, in hindsight, was a sordid affair. Two months after his release, he returned to his marriage, and he and poor Edith strived to make their amends.

For the second time in no time, he had made a sorry decision – as Parnell made it clear, their love was still true. Faltering perhaps but only a moment, he stood by his decision – and suffered her wrath.

The scorned woman, Parnell was convinced of her problem – 'old' Edith Hopwood had got in her way. Parnell daubed graffiti and threw bricks through the window; but soon she decided she needed an edge…

Catching hold of her rival as they passed on the pavement, she attacked Edith Hopwood and warned her away. Her rival in love was not so easily frightened – Hopwood left the young woman sprawled out on the floor.

Thus the troubles continued, with scarce interruption, until the women and Hopwood landed in court. Charged with keeping the peace or spending time in the prison, Parnell stepped up her efforts to put Edith away…

Edward M'Auliffe, police constable, was the first to bear witness:

On 2 December, at about six in the evening, he was called to a house on the west side of town. Inside was Parnell, in a great state of excitement, stretched out as though fatally wounded and displaying the signs of an insensible mind.

'Oh, George, George, don't!' She seemed quite incoherent. 'George Hopwood, George Hopwood, I done you no harm!'

A woman named Dearn, whose rooms he had entered, had seen the attack outside her front door. The assailants, she said – and later backed-up by the 'victim' – had covered their faces but she knew who they were.

Acting on details they subsequently gave him, M'Auliffe led Dearn to the address she had sworn. He informed Mr Hopwood of his wife's alleged misdemeanour, and arrested poor Edith for common assault.

Instead of taking her round to a cell in the station, he marched both women back and confronted Parnell.

'Is this the assailant?' he asked of the 'victim'.

'Yes,' she agreed, '*That* is the woman!' and quickly 'collapsed' from the weight of her 'pain'.

The surgeon, Benjamin Vale, thought her injuries nasty, but never so fatal that they threatened her life. The cuts on her neck he remembered were shallow – no more than skin deep, however so caused. He dismissed the lines on her throat as no sign of a struggle; they were too rigidly straight for a violent attack.

If not an assault, then what had possibly caused them?

A fork, he concluded, or perhaps a *trebat* – a tool used by weavers for parting their fabric.

A common appliance?

He suggested it was.

He was asked if he knew how Parnell earned her money?
  A weaver, he answered, at least that's what she had told him.

The questions then changed, to discuss her condition. He insisted hysterics was the malady felt. Unable to speak, except in a struggle, her '*hysterical feelings*' were easy to see.

Mrs Dormer, the landlady, who had joined the commotion, recalled Parnell's incoherence as she lay on the floor. If Parnell felt smug, it rapidly left her as Dormer reported what she had seen.
  Parnell's hysteria had then only lasted till Dearn was despatched to fetch the police. As soon as she left, Parnell had recovered and was 'perfectly sane' until M'Auliffe walked in!

While under attack from Edith Hopwood's attorney, first Dearn, then Parnell, failed to stick to their tales:

Defence: 'Are you any relation to Mrs Parnell?'

Dearn: 'None at all; I am quite sure about that. I am the wife of Mr Dearn.'

Court (Justice Talfourd): 'Were you married in a Church? You say you consider that you are the lawful wife of Dearn, were you married to him in a Church?'

Dearn: 'No sir; not in a Church.'

Defence: 'On the solemn oath you have taken to tell the truth, and recollect you can be punished if you tell a falsehood, were you ever married at all to the man Dearn?'

Dearn: 'We are on the point of marriage—that is telling you the truth.'

Defence: 'So you say.'

Dearn: 'I am his lawful wife. I say that on my oath. I consider myself his lawful wife. I am his lawful wife. I was married; I do not know the Church. I am just turned twenty-five years of age; I have been married two years and three weeks. I do not know the Church where I was married.'

Defence needed no proof that Dearn's words were a lie.

Now Parnell, faced with questions, became unsure of the story:

Defence: 'Do you work at a weaver's shop?'

Parnell: 'I work up in a shop; there are no weavers in the shop, nor any in the house.'

Defence: 'You do not work in a weaver's shop?'

Parnell: 'There are no weavers in the house; I work in a shop.'

Defence: 'Do you work in a weaver's shop?'

Parnell: 'Not that I know of; I cannot say whether it is a weaver's or not.'

Defence: 'Are there any weavers' shops about there?'

Parnell: 'There are no weavers that I am acquainted with—there are weavers about there; a great many.'

Dearn was questioned again (though now an unreliable witness). She 'confirmed' what the surgeon had said about Parnell's complaint:

'She was almost out of her senses – she exclaimed, "Oh, Sarah, Sarah! Mrs Hopwood has cut my throat".'

As the courtroom erupted, the jury 'retired'; delivering their verdict in no time at all. Edith Hopwood – NOT GUILTY – all charges rejected. No case to answer – it had always been lies.

The clerk demanded absolute silence; Justice Talfourd called Dearn and Parnell to the floor. They were told to appear, at the next Old Bailey sessions – each charged with *lying while under an oath*!

Courtroom Hysterics; or Trial – the second

Parnell stood, on 3 February,* in the spot where her rival had escaped a capital charge. After a short confirmation of her earlier promise [oath], the typographer

---

* Sarah Dearn was tried for perjury at the following Sessions. She too was found guilty and sent to Newgate for 24 months.

read out what her impeachments had been (*see above*). The witnesses were then recalled to appear – and it was quickly apparent she was out on her own.

In her previous statements, Parnell had long laboured, her claim of hysterics from Hopwood's attack. She now used her distress to explain a lack of awareness of the events at the time now related in court. [These included Dormer's assertion that her neck wound was minor [more a scratch than a cut]; and how she recovered her mind until M'Auliffe walked in.]

The surgeon, Vale, made an uncomfortable witness. When examined once more, he defended his stance:

'I took no means of ascertaining whether her insensibility was feigned or not, [as] I thought it was real.'

When asked if the wound could have caused her hysterics, he agreed that it did, or rather it might:

'… from the wounds being [made], and … the excitement [it caused].'

Then he described his numerous visits, which he made to the woman in the following days. When repeatedly grilled, about her condition, he admitted not everything was once what it seemed:

'[S]he had her senses, but being in a debilitated state from previous excitement, she required some time to think before she answered a question…[yes,] there was a great deal of hysteria about her.'

When asked to explain, he could hardly continue:

'Such hysteria would account for a person speaking a few words … but she would not be able to carry on a conversation.'

And acknowledged that:

'[H]ysteria can be assumed, and frequently is, but I was called suddenly in, and my impression was, that she was insensible from real causes.'

At this point, the insanity plea may have flashed through his senses, but with no more witness to call, the jury retired. They again took no time in reaching their verdict. GUILTY of perjury, with malicious intent.

What Next for Hell's Fury?

Jane Parnell – a scorned lover, who had faked her hysterics – was given eight days in Newgate; it could have been worse. As she sighed with relief, the judge carried on speaking – she was going to be transported for a full seven *years*!

On 22 April, she set sail for Tasmania [Van Diemen's Land], aboard the vessel, *Aurora* on a trip lasting three months. As she no doubt resolved to make the most of her journey, the Hopwoods went home and got on with their lives.

James Pownall – *A Lunatic in Charge of the Asylum*

Tuesday 30 August 1859 – Murder; Homicidal Mania, Lydney, Gloucestershire
James Pownall was a product of the Victorian system – magistrate, mayor and practising surgeon. Most notably, he was Superintendent of his asylum in Calne (Wiltshire), where he undoubtedly treated the criminally insane. Over time, it proved good preparation.

In c.1829, when aged just 22, Pownall suffered his own first attack of irrational violence. With hindsight, it was a sign of his problems to come. A second event, some fourteen years later, saw him 'murder' a man while out shooting one day. Though the coroner returned an accidental verdict, others believed the truth lay deep in his mind.

Assault and Pepper
By 1859, Pownall was a doctor. Married and living with his wife, sister and his wife's 80-year-old mother, to casual observers his life was complete. But about Easter that year, his violent behaviour would quickly resurface and shatter the peace …

Grabbing a poker, he beat the old woman, in what was later described as a 'vicious assault'. As he rained down blow after blow on the fragile woman, it seemed nothing would stop him until she was dead. Defying the odds, she somehow survived – and Pownall, for now, faced no capital charge.

Attending the scene, Dr Morris found his colleague 'insensible' – having swallowed some chloroform, intending to die. It had, though, left him only poisoned and vacant, with no long-term effect on his disordered mind.

When challenged for answers, he complained the woman 'annoyed him', that she had recently caused him pecuniary pain. Whatever the truth, the family wanted him 'sectioned', and tasked the good doctor with finding a way.

Keen to avoid washing their linen in public, Morris brought in a medic he knew they could trust. Pownall would be sent to Dr Davey's asylum [Northwoods, near Bristol]; and the best of it was, no-one need ever know.

Waiting to go, and while sitting with wardens, Pownall took umbrage at their careless remarks. Excusing himself for a pitcher of water, he made off to the room where his shotgun was stored.

Keeping the weapon from view, he rushed to where the three women sat talking, raised it up to his shoulder and threatened to pepper them all. Only his sister's resolve averted disaster, as she grabbed hold of the muzzle and aimed it up in the air.

The next day, 2 April, Pownall was removed to Davey's asylum.

Administrative Failings

After only four months, Dr Davey exclaimed Pownall was fully recovered – suggesting his condition had been only short-lived. *Homicidal mania* (*see Part 2*) could be checked until his demeanour was settled. Awaiting release, Davey contacted his wife.

The family resisted, no-one wanted him home now; the danger was too great, he could have murdered them all. But, argued Davey, he needed reintegration – besides, he had no legal reason to keep him confined.

They insisted he be sent to Stafford's Coton Hill asylum [for reasons unknown] – when Davey refused, they sought an answer in law. Approaching the Lunacy Commission (*see Part 1*), who agreed with Davey's assessment, they ordered release if not sent out alone.

Davey arranged with a professional colleague – a surgeon called Leete in the Forest of Dean. Pownall would stay at his practice in Lydney, while a keeper from Northwoods [Richard Pooke] would be sent to attend.

Davey had found an uneasy solution; but at least James Pownall was out of his hands. Unfortunately, Davey made a series of administrative errors – that would lead to the patient's worst offence yet.

In August, he was sent with two pieces of paper. The first, a certificate, was simple enough:

'Northwoods, near Bristol, 10th of August, 1859. I hereby certify that Mr Pownall has been under my care here for some four months, that he is now quite recovered, and is this day discharged cured.'

It was signed: 'J.G. Davey, M.D.'

(JPM 13: xiv)

The second, a letter, was meant for Leete and, according to Davey, should have put the man on his guard. Where Davey appears to have abandoned his duty was in not *posting* both papers himself, or entrusting them to Pooke.

Instead, he gave them to Pownall – the one man he should not have – as a medic himself, he knew they could constitute proof!

[When asked later why he had not sent both *direct* to Leete, Davey confessed he thought it would cheer Pownall up – to know he was trusted would suggest he was cured.].

The repercussions were tragic, the outcome long-lasting; as the note contained hints to keep everyone safe. Davey had written of one particular danger: not to let Pownall near razors in the following weeks.

Murder!

In less than a fortnight, Pownall declared himself better – and, as Davey had written, he was now a free man. He confirmed his intention to travel to London, to attend to some business he had to transact.

Pooke was sent back to Northwoods Asylum, while Pownall remained in the company of Leete. But as soon as the warder had set off for Bristol, Pownall announced that he needed a shave.

On 30 August, seven days later, Pownall and a servant were alone in the house. Engaged in debate, talking of things that upset him, he collected his razor and slashed the girl's throat (eg *JPM* 13: xiii) …

Murderous Outcry

Pownall stood trial at the Gloucester Assizes, but was quickly acquitted on account of his mind. The law, it seemed – unlike Dr Davey in Bristol – refused to take chances and declared him insane.

Now kept at Her Majesty's Pleasure, he arrived into Bethlem on 9 January. The man would never again experience freedom; as his family had said, the risk was too great.

The murderous outcry – at the shambles leading up to the killing – appeared in the press and far beyond court. In-fighting alienists endorsed rife condemnation: the case brought immeasurable damage in their fight for their cause.

Loudest among them was the outspoken Winslow; the comments he made caught the mood at the time. Davey, he claimed, had acted in fear of reprisal, from public discomfort with the insanity plea.

Judges, juries and medics especially were pilloried for attempting to 'declare' sane men mad. Whether for 'unrighteous admission' to their private asylums, or to keep the guilty from hanging on a capital charge. Dr Davey, it seemed, declared Pownall a free man, because his wrongful confinement would have seen him arraigned. As Winslow lamented, straight after the trial:

'It might [be] expected, as a natural result of the tendency of public feeling, that the proprietors of asylums would become very chary of detaining a lunatic one moment longer under care than was absolutely [allowed]' (*JPM* 13: xiv-xv).

A Late Diagnosis?

Mr Hood, Medical Superintendent at Bethlem Hospital, contested that James Pownall's condition was something unknown. Indeed, were he not held as a *criminal* lunatic, it would have been hard to keep him detained.

Henry Maudsley, meanwhile – the alienist juggernaut – chipped in with his thoughts on the general point (1896: 140–43). Doubtless with one eye to the law, he said that Pownall had suffered rabid *delusions* – and murdered the girl after an imaginary slight. 'Homicidal maniacs', he added, usually contained their illusions until, at times of great violence, they were allowed to break out.

He cited the earlier outbursts of Pownall's aggression as times when this malady might well have occurred. It was hard to condemn – as a responsible agent – when *irresistible impulse* [to kill] might have overwhelmed his resolve:

'We shall not be in a position to form a right judgment concerning any case of this kind unless we distinctly realize the possibility of an impulse to violence in an unbound mind becoming at times perfectly uncontrollable' (*ibid*: 143).

James Pownall, still an inmate – though now transferred to Broadmoor – died on 11 December 1882. Many observed how he never again displayed signs of his madness … though no-one had been happy to chance a release.

Richard Pritchard/Rebecca Turton – *Insane on Arraignment*

Featuring two short cases that highlight the confusion – and dangers – of finding the prisoner Insane on Arraignment.

'A Visitation of God'
Richard Pritchard, March 1836 – Bestiality; Unfit To Plead, Shrewsbury

The case of Richard Pritchard, 28, a deaf-and-dumb mute, occurred fifteen months before Queen Victoria's accession. Yet its ramifications were felt long after her death. Though his crime was largely uncommon, it was his 'fitness to plead' that led to a change in the law.

Little is known of Pritchard's earlier years. In 1834, he may have stood trial before the Shrewsbury Sessions (Quarter Sessions), where a man with his name faced a larceny charge. Whatever the truth, two years later, Richard Pritchard appeared 'again' …

On 21 March, at the Lent Shrewsbury Assizes, he stood trial for an altogether more troubling crime. Bestiality (sex with an animal) was seen then, as now, in inhuman terms. [Clerks of the day 'sanitised' his crime to the (still illicit) sodomy act.]

Before the 'Bloody Code' changed (see *Glossary*), his crime attracted a capital sentence, though he was unlikely to suffer such barbarous wrath. Then, even before the hearing got going, a more challenging matter troubled the court.

Was Pritchard, a 'mute', fit to stand trial – when his affliction prevented him making his plea?

Fitness To Plead
Presiding judge, Baron Alderson, addressed the conundrum, drawing on Hadfield's case and the subsequent law (*see Appendix 2*). There were, he revealed, three steps to consider, which he spelt out to court in the following terms.

First, he empanelled the jury to decide on his silence – was Pritchard 'mute of malice or from the visitation of God' [ie was he genuinely affected or putting it on]? Witnesses were called to attest his *natural* affliction – an opinion the jury was happy to take.

Second, could Pritchard enter a plea without talking? His known education [taught to read and write by the Deaf and Dumb Asylum (*sic*)] meant the written indictment could be passed to the dock. By making a sign, Pritchard pleaded not guilty – allowing the trial to continue, at least to stage three.

The third issue demanded: was he fit to stand trial – was he sufficiently sane to grasp what would happen in court? Unlike the plea, it proved more controversial, as the judge and the jury were destined to see.

Fit to Stand Trial

There were a number of points where he could be considered a madman, either at the time of the crime [found not guilty on account of his mind]; or since his arrest [placed on remand until judged to be sane – a rare event, but *see Turton below*]. He might yet be found *Insane on Arraignment* (*see Glossary*) – a double-edged sword of mercy and risk (cf Davies, *Part 5*).

What's more, as a mute, he was in the 'idiot' classes, an image not weakened by the form of his crime:

> '[w]e do not know whether those accused of bestiality were abnormally incapacitated in intellect, or whether it was a poor rural background, not to mention the nature of the crime itself, which led their being defined idiotic' (Smith 1981a: 93).

With no clear guidelines on how to move forward, Alderson opted for the following words:

> 'Is the defendant of sufficient intellect to comprehend the course of proceedings on the trial, so as to make a proper defence? To know that he might challenge any of you to whom he may object? And to comprehend the details of the evidence, *which in a case of this nature must constitute a minute investigation?*' (in Walker 1968: 225, my *emphasis*).

It became 'the most authoritative definition of the test of [the defendant's] *fitness to plead*' (*ibid*) – one that was still being used a century on.

Alderson continued:

> 'Upon this issue, therefore, if you think that there is no certain mode of communicating the details of the trial to the prisoner, so that he can clearly understand them, and be able properly to make his defence to the charge; you ought to find that he is not of sane mind' (7 *C&P*: 304–05).

Adding:

> 'It is not enough, that he may have a general capacity of communicating on
> ordinary matters' (*ibid*: 305).

Prosecution witnesses now testified that Pritchard was capable of understanding
the hearing. He had done so, of course, at the [earlier] magistrate's court. There
he had *written* his answers when bombarded with questions. What could stop
him from doing so over again?

Others though argued firmly against it – he is 'very nearly an idiot', as classed
by the law. 'Though he might be able to be made to comprehend some [salient]
matters, yet he could not understand the proceedings [in court]' (*ibid*: 304).

Judgements and Repercussions

As ever, the jury were tasked with resolving the issue: aware their decision could
affect the man's life. If they found him *Insane on Arraignment*, he could be kept
under His Majesty's Pleasure (ie *ad infinitum*, though never convicted); if *Fit to
Stand Trial*, he could be hanged. They deduced that the man might have shown
fitness in pleading (through signing), but he remained, in their view, unfit to
stand trial.

Alderson duly ordered Pritchard's detention.

Afterwords

But where was he kept? How long his detention? The records confirm he was
sent back to gaol. Soon after, he moved to the local asylum, though it was never
made clear how long he was there. That it was a temporary stay is verified later,
when Richard Pritchard again appeared in court.

In 1841, charged with stealing some flour, his trial was again interrupted
when they found him insane. It seems reasonable to assume he went back to
where he came from – though still not *convicted* of committing a crime.

* * *

'Double Jeopardy'

Rebecca Turton, Friday 21–Saturday 22 April 1854 – Murder; Unfit to Plead/Undiagnosed Insanity, Poplar/Bromley, Kent

Rebecca Turton, 22, became a rare legal example, twice placed in court for the very same crime. First she was found *Insane on Arraignment*, then appeared again having 'recovered' her mind. This time thought sane enough to stand trial, she ignited debates on the '*Burden of Proof*'.

A Mind For A Crime

In the early hours of 21 April 1854, PC Pulling [Pullen?] was called to 1 St Peter's Street, Bromley in the county of Kent. William Walker, a landlord, had reported Turton, his lodger – after the latter informed him her husband was dead. When both men found Thomas, asleep in their bedroom, the dazed man exclaimed: 'I do not know what to do with my wife.' Then added, with feeling: 'I [swear] she is mad!' (*The Times* 23 August 1854).

Thirty minutes later, when Pulling was passing, Rebecca threw up the window and called out his name. 'Are you the Devil?!' she shouted. 'The cats are scratching the graves open!' But Pulling just sighed and said she should return to her bed (*Old Bailey Proceedings Online*).

The following morning, he was again called to the lodgings; though this time they found Thomas Turton was dead. His head had been placed on a feather-down pillow, while Rebecca kept pacing till he told her to stop. In reply, she beseeched him. 'I did not do it!' as she cried out in anguish, then said it again (*ibid*).

Burden of Proof

Within hours, Turton appeared before the Magistrate, Ingham; charged with Thomas' death, having 'strangled his throat'. The murder weapon was one of his braces, which left a buckle impression at the top of his jaw.

Turton was indicted to stand trial for murder and briefly appeared at the Old Bailey court. The hearing in May took just a few minutes, the burden of proof (*see Glossary*) had got in the way.

Unlike Pritchard the mute, and David Davies the Elder (*see Part 5*), Justice Cresswell said Turton should prove she was mad.

Mr Sleigh (Turton's unhappy counsel) requested adjournment – his client was clearly insane and unable to plead.

Cresswell retorted, it was up to her counsel, to prove what he said had a basis in fact. If he did not feel able, to put proof on the table, he could sanction no chances of further delay:

Cresswell: 'Mr Sleigh, you suggest that the prisoner is insane. Do you offer any evidence?'

Sleigh: 'I submit that I am not obliged to do so. The prosecution should prove her sanity. Regina versus David Davies [*see Part 5*] ... is in point. In that case the learned judge decided that it was the duty of the counsel for the prosecution to prove the prisoner's sanity and capability to plead.'

Cresswell: 'Why is a man to be presumed insane when called upon to plead? The presumption is that he is sane. I do not see any sufficient reason for deviating from the old practice. If you suggest that the prisoner is not in such a state of mind as to be able to plead to the indictment, you must give evidence of the fact.'

(taken from 6 *Cox C C*)

No doubt in deference to his place in the courtroom, Sleigh called three witnesses to attest to the claim. All had shown an interest in Turton, while held on remand in Newgate next door.

Mr McMurdo, the Medical Officer, and Mr Wilders, his deputy, were convinced she had no recollection of committing a crime. While Reverend Davis, the Ordinary (Chaplain), spoke of her claims to know Satan, and how her husband had 'rubbed her all over with a white powder, and had [driven] her mad' (*The Times* 12 May 1854).

The jury – easily led or on base intuition – thought her unfit to plead and declared her insane.

Barely concealing his simmering anger, Cresswell now ordered she must be detained. Until Her Majesty's Pleasure be known (in practice, the Home Secretary's intentions), and was brought back to court to stand trial again.

What A Journey

At this point, Turton was 'remanded' to Newgate. Five weeks later – on 15 June – she went to Bethlem Hospital, where she remained for six more. At the end of July, she went to Fisherton House, on the outskirts of Salisbury – the largest criminal asylum used at the time.

By the end of May 1855, a full ten months later, the Home Secretary's decision brought the case back to court. Not content to leave her under Her Majesty's Pleasure, he ordered her trial should be started once more.

The Insanity Plea

Having previously been found *Insane on Arraignment*, the one option left open was the insanity plea. In short, that she was mad at the time of the killing – whether or not she was anymore.

On 20 August, back at the Old Bailey, the Bench now demanded she enter a plea [*not guilty*]. The full extent of her madness, as declared by her counsel, would soon test the jury sworn in to decide.

James Green, a key witness, recalled Turton's behaviour, in the days that preceded the hideous crime. She claimed Thomas, her husband, had been trying to kill her – and spoke of four men and a yacht that were to take her to sea. He admitted, back then, he had considered her tipsy; then added, in fact, he had thought she was mad.

Ann Randall, the female searcher at the local police station, now related her talk when Rebecca came in:

Randall: 'Was your husband a good husband to you?'

Turton: 'Very good, when he is sober.'

Randall: 'It is a very bad thing it should have happened.'

Turton: 'Certainly it was a bad thing, but what will not the devil tempt a person to do when they are in a passion?'

(*Old Bailey Proceedings Online*)

Toward the end of the hearing, McMurdo confirmed he had taken charge of the prisoner, when she was sent back from Fisherton ahead of the trial. He was as adamant now of what he claimed was her *saneness*, as he had thought her quite mad only twelve months before. Although he accepted she still had no recollection of murder, he could offer no reason why she should have avoided the stand.

Finally, Hannah Connor, a girl with whom Turton was friendly, revealed how she came to her house and said Thomas was dead. As the two women returned to the scene of the horror, she said fairies and corpses were lining the road.

Verdicts …

The jury returned a verdict of proven insanity, or not guilty by virtue of her weakness of mind. What followed revealed much about the administrative headaches an acquittal like hers caused the law at the time.

In September, she was returned to the hospital at Bethlem, five months later once more into Fisherton House.* Where, in a turn of events, she went from patient to witness in a historical case even rarer than hers.

… and Endings

In June 1858, Turton recounted a murder – of inmate killing inmate, while left unwisely alone. 'CC' [Catherine Clarke] struck 'MK' [Mary Kenney] with the point of an iron, and finished her off with the sole of her boot (www.wiltshire-opc.org.uk/).

Five years later, though sane enough to be a reliable witness, she was transferred to the new Criminal Lunatic Asylum at Crowthorne in Berks. One of the first (all female) inmates, she entered Broadmoor's surroundings, to remain a further six years until faced with more change.

In August that year [1869], she was discharged as sane and recovered; this time the authorities felt they need not do more. Some fifteen years after killing her husband, Rebecca Turton was let free and returned to the world.

Through *Insanity on Arraignment* and then a plea of insanity, she had escaped first the gallows then institutionalisation for life. Not everyone then was always that 'lucky' – but such were the vagaries of pleading insane.

---

* This detained her in the same institution, the same wing, likely the *very same ward*, as Celestina Sommer, reported elsewhere – *see Part 5*.

Amelia G. Snoswell – *'I have killed her – I have made her happy'*

Tuesday 13 August 1850 – Murdered Her Niece; 'Homicidal Insanity from Disordered Menstruation', Milton, Kent

By murdering her niece, Amelia Snoswell entered the rumpus on how best to handle women who killed (*see Part 4*). The insanity plea and its myriad 'causes' (*see Part 2*) used her womb, menstruation and so-called 'monthly attack'. Mercurial medics and uncertain lawyers brought an unusual outcome in a Victorian court.

[All quotes below are taken from (various) contemporary reports (see bibliography).]

On the 13 August 1850, in Milton near Gravesend in Kent, Amelia G. Snoswell (she was very particular about her middle initial) – just 20 years old and a governess full-time – made one of her frequent visits to her sister and family. All knew why she came, not just from love for her sibling; it was the baby she cherished, not having her own. Thirteen months old, her reason to visit: 'Dear Alice', 'My Alice'; wasn't that what she thought?

Late in the evening, Mrs Hooper, their mother, nursed the children at bedtime, before returning downstairs. After waiting a while, Amelia muttered excuses, climbed the stairs to the nursery and entered the room.

A few minutes later she appeared on the landing; something was wrong. As she called out for help, a knife hung from her hand – the sort held back for carving. Both it and Amelia were coated in blood.

'I have killed her,' she shouted, unsure if they heard her. 'I have made her [quite] happy,' she said with a smile.

Her sister rushed past, were the children still sleeping? But she broke down in tears at the horror inside.

The older child was unharmed, his sleep easing his breathing. But Alice, dear Alice, lay as still as could be. Her throat had been cut, the wound was still bleeding – an artery severed, the girl now at peace.

In the melee that followed, Amelia tried to get back to the children, but her brother-in-law held her back with a force. 'Let me go to my child!' Their father resisted. 'Let me go to my Alice!' Then said it again …

A Long Trail for Answers

From the night of arrest, to seven months later, Amelia was kept in Kent County Gaol, in Maidstone, fifty miles from home. Her only visitors, it seemed, were her desperate counsel, and medical attendants tasked with assessing her mind …

Their aim was to find examples of 'madness' – though surely the act was enough to prove that! Yet they uncovered enough to have suggested a problem – these alienist 'experts' had hit on a 'truth'.

The attack came during her menstrual cycle – not only that, it had not been the first. She had often – the *London Medical Gazette* published later – suffered 'a constitutional irregularity, likely to [torment] the brain' (1851: 569).

In the days of growing concern for a woman's 'emotional weakness', and a burgeoning sympathy for women who killed, amenorrhoea was increasingly cited to excuse their behaviour of the most horrid sort.

Alienists like Prichard (1837) and, with him, T Laycock (1840), had published their treatises on nervous decay. *Irresistible impulse* was said to pardon a murder – Snoswell's assault could be seen in this way.

The case of Martha Brixey (*see Part 5*), just five years earlier, was cited as proof that their theories were right. A menstruating woman suffered emotional disruption that weakened her nerves and unsettled her mind.

Far from being universally accepted, such brave new opinion ignited the fire that fuelled the debates. But, others maintained, a mad woman's body could have acted without the control of her mind.

For Snoswell, the alienists uncovered a reason – the explanation they sought for her turbulent mind. An engagement to marry was ended a few months prior to the murder – leaving her anxious, unsettled and emotionally drained. In her efforts to die, she swallowed oxalic acid – a violent attempt to permanently end all the pain. And though she survived, it was the proof they had needed as to why she murdered the innocent girl.

Of course, what mattered now was whether they and their 'theories' were accepted in court.

The World Has Been Watching

Amelia Snoswell stood trial at the local Assizes, but things soon got off to a terrible start. Presiding judge, Baron Parke was regarded the harshest of critics, and well known to the world for his unbending approach.

Her counsel however, appointed by favour, was Bodkin, a barrister not unused to the insanity plea (cf *Celestina Sommer, Part 5*). Unusually for him, Parke allowed his medical 'experts' – not a foregone conclusion in crimes of this kind.

Speaking of proof of Amelia's madness, they explained to the jury its 'probable' cause. The defendant, they claimed, had suffered '*homicidal insanity – depending on disordered menstruation*', of the very worst sort.

As the specialist witnesses concluded their statements, an unusual event was seen to occur. The foreman stood up and begged His Honour for mercy … the jury was sure the defendant was mad!

[As a point of conjecture, Baron Parke should have resisted the crass interruption, and insisted all witnesses and evidence be heard. But whether displaying compassion – untrue to his manner – this 'harshest of barons' accepted their call.]

As a formality, maybe, he asked him to confirm their decision.

'Not Guilty,' he said, on account of her mind.

Snoswell was led from the dock to the prison. Under Her Majesty's Pleasure (*see Glossary*), she awaited more news …

An Unforeseen Turn

Kent's Barming Asylum had opened its doors some 18 years earlier. By the time Snoswell arrived, new wings housed inmates of Amelia's kind. Arriving from gaol on 17 April, she lived in relative comfort to the one she had left behind.

After only eight years, her 'correction' saw an unforeseen ending. Though to many, it simply confirmed what they knew. In these days of a queen seen to favour her gender, the registers' entries recorded the news:

'Amelia G. Snoswell, discharged as recovered, *by order of the Queen*!'

While only, in truth, a formal quotation, she was released nonetheless, the blood washed from her hands. No record has shown how her family reacted … but her sentence was shorter than many had hoped for.

The events of spring 1866 proved equally shocking. One Amelia G. Snoswell married a printer named Hull. Five years later, the 1871 census reveals that they lived in Portugal Street, London – near Lincoln's Inn Fields. Her occupation was shown as a 'Law Copyist' function, and one wonders if Bodkin had in any way helped.

Ten years later, they resided in Lambeth, and Amelia is listed as a 'clergyman's keeper'. Whether spared by the law or saved by religion, her respectable living had shrouded her past.

A 'Lucky Escape'

Since her trial, Snoswell owed her life to the alienists and jury – and their oft-criticised views of women who killed. That Baron Parke entertained the insanity 'ticket' shows the importance of gender in Victorian courts. Whether from bad menstruation or difficult births, the taste for punishing women had lost its appeal.

Celestina Sommer – *A Very Victorian Error?*

Saturday 16 February 1856 – Murdered Her Daughter; Non-Diagnosed Insanity, Islington, Middlesex

> *'Few instances of more unrelenting cruelty have [ever] been recorded'*
> (HC Deb 10 June 1856 vol 142 cols 1231–261)

Celestina Sommer was the devilish problem of a Victorian obsession with madness and crime. Charged with the murder of her own 10-year-old daughter, her 'cunning' and methods were unspeakably cruel. Found sane – and thus guilty – and sentenced to hanging, the nation erupted when her life was then spared. Certainly saved by George Grey, through his Home Secretary's Mercy (*see Glossary*), rumours soon started it was brought by the Queen.

December 1845
Celestina Sommer (née Christmas) did what she could to conceal the birth of her daughter. Just 18 years old, with few legitimate options, she took a desperate decision and hoped it would work. The baby-farmers of London may have attracted a poor reputation, but if she could find one 'half-decent', it might yet save the day. Weeks later, in what must have been an act of defiance, she named her daughter Celestina – the same as her own.

February 1856
As the years rolled by, now dutifully married, her past indiscretion brought misery still. Her husband, Karl Sommer, a die-cutter from Prussia, had once accepted her error but not any more. Objecting to paying the 'maintenance' payments, his response to the problem was found in his fists.

With what many said later was malice aforethought, she desperately sought answers in haphazard ways. On February 7, she collected her daughter from her surrogate family, who had cared for the girl since the day she was born. With no solution to work to, she placed the girl with her sister – the child could stay there while she thought what to do.

Saturday morning, 16 February, she took the child to the canal with a box and a brick. But, for whatever reason, she abandoned the plan. Yet about seven that night, she found her solution – with her husband out for the evening, she had to work fast. Again retrieving the girl, who had gone back to her sister, she led her back across London to her Islington house.

Changing her clothes, she led the girl to the cellar, but paused for a knife she thought would do the job well. In no time at all, though the girl put up a struggle, Celestina had butchered her throat and left her to die.

The next morning, unsure how to rid herself of the body, she left the dead child to be found by the maid. The Linton Street horror, quite unlike any other, would inflame the debates on women who killed.

Public Persona, Private Dismay

By the time Celestina stood trial at the Old Bailey, she was the most reviled woman of the Victorian age. In less than 24 hours, she was the most evil of mothers, a devilish taker of innocent souls. The press roared its contempt, confirmed what others were thinking, and the public accepted the tales they were told.

After a magistrates' hearing that drew thousands of people, she faced the Old Bailey judge with no hope of reprieve. No insanity plea was ever suggested, nor alienists present to offer its means. Besides, worst of all, she had 'inveigled' her victim – a popular measure of an *all-knowing* mind (cf Rules, *Appendix 3*). *Puerperal* [post-natal] *madness* (*see Part 4*) was never an option chiefly because of her dead daughter's age.

Instead, Ballantine, her counsel, plied a desperate measure: her husband's violent behaviour had disordered her mind. In outright disgust and vilification, she was found guilty of murder and sentenced to hang.

How On Earth Did She Do It?

When, on the day of her hanging, she was saved from the gallows – her sentence commuted to prison for life – an outraged response would soon bring disquiet, especially with rumours the queen was involved. Amidst claims of corruption and racist conjecture, there remained just the one incontrovertible truth – both she and the killer were married to Germans – to 'murder' their own would simply not do.

More scandal now formed around her escape as a woman: too pretty, too tender, too fragile to hang.* While Grey, the Home Secretary, was said to be hamstrung – by a second young mother on trial the same day. As others would claim, there could be no slaughter of mothers, and to reprieve one, not the other, left the minister caught.

Cause célèbre

In the ongoing debates about crime and insanity, she quickly invoked a clamour for change. In his letter to *The Times*, dated 22 December, Thomas Mayo (*see Part 1*) voiced the fears of a nation left torn:

> 'the relaxation which has been conceded of late to capital punishment in relation to presumed irregularity of mind has further loosened the moral hold which society once had upon its more atrocious delinquents... The impunity of Celestina Sommer ... has satisfied a large number of garrotters, and burglars, and sentimental murderers, [so] that the "quality of mercy" is somewhat "strained" in the present day.'

Away from the press, in the corridors of power, questions were asked in both the Commons and Lords. Mr Samuel Warren, Member of Parliament for Midhurst in Sussex [and future Lunacy Master],** tabled a question that only brought scorn:

> 'whether the advisers of the Crown, in recommending a commutation of the sentence of death lately passed on Celestina Somner (*sic*), at the Central Criminal Court, for the murder of her child, had obtained the Report and taken the opinion of the Judge [Justice Crompton] by whom she had been tried; and, if so, whether there was any objection to laying them before the House?' (HC Deb 20 May 1856 vol 142 col 428)

---

*   Reports described her as 'an exceedingly pretty woman – a *blonde* – with very pointed features ...' (*emphasis* original – *Empire* 23 February 1856).

** Masters in Lunacy heard cases of *de lunatico inquirendo*, in which an accused lunatic's property and welfare became subject to a Chancery Court.

The Bishop of Oxford demanded an answer – did Sommer's reprieve spell the end of punishing 'girls'? Yet others decried not just the decision, but how it occurred behind ministerial doors.

The Home Secretary told him his reasons were secret – to say any more would bring shame on them all.

With the passage of time, and unwarranted fortune, he must have welcomed the news that was soon to explode. With no proof of madness to justify pardon, he must have felt some relief from Sommer's decline.

A Descent Into Madness

Following her passage through several prisons – from Newgate to Millbank, then Brixton, the last – her mind weakened daily, so clear was her madness that after thirty-six months she was recorded insane.

Arriving at Fisherton House, Salisbury, by the following April [1859], she died of an illness that ruptured her brain. A post-mortem revealed, to the government's comfort, her reasons for murder were one and the same:

> '[twenty-seven] hours after death the vessels of the brain were found to be injected with blood to a very abnormal extent and there was also considerable effusion of serum on the surface of the brain and in the ventricles the brain in some portions was somewhat softened but no other morbid appearances were visible the viscera of the chest and abdomen were not examined' (WSHC).

Such a condition, perhaps, the alienists argued, was a plausible cause of her earlier state. Compare her post-mortem notes with the following passage – the *physicalist* theory (*see Part 2*) had been given its wings:

> 'The most important empirical argument for physicalism came from post-mortem examinations of brains, surrounding membranes and connected blood vessels.' Thus: '"In the great majority of persons *dying insane*, the cerebral organs present distinctive appearances which can be readily appreciated"' (in Smith 1981a: 44, my *emphasis*).

Did Celestina Sommer, then, have a cause for her madness? Had an unhealthy brain made her act as she did? Was this revelation in death the one real reason – one Grey could have shared if only he'd known?

Continued Objections

Seven years later, her notorious hearing was used once again in a crucial debate. Referencing the Home Secretary's inexplicable decision, the *Royal Commission on Capital Punishment* soon cited the press:

> 'The murder of her two children by Elizabeth Harris, a double murder, presents no one feature which can suggest that her sentence exceeded the requirements of justice, and the slaughter of her child by Celestina Sommer ranks as one of the most deliberate and cruel murders ever recorded. The dissatisfaction long felt by the public at the uncertainty of the sentences of the Courts of Justice, and the still greater uncertainty whether the sentences passed [death] would be really inflicted, was greatly raised. It was felt that this indecision had reduced our judicial punishments to a lottery, in which the criminal who drew a bad ticket was very unlucky indeed' (HMSO 1868: 194).

The former Home Secretary was forced to remember a case he would clearly have liked to forget. As he highlighted the hardships of excusing a killer, who from the limits of law, had no insanity plea:

> 'I have not mentioned one case which was *not, strictly speaking, child murder*, but the well-known case of a woman named Celestina Sommers (*sic*), who murdered a child ten years old, but the sentence was not commuted on the ground of its being infanticide, the commutation was on the ground of her supposed insanity...' (HMSO 1866 (5): 192, my *emphasis*).

Explanation – or Symptom?

When Celestina's baby was born, only she knew the father: the one other person who brought the girl to the world. That person was William ... her own elder brother ... who had died when their daughter was still very young:

> '"It is my brother's child. He is dead now and I promised to keep it. I have been paying five shillings a week for its support. I did not like to put her

out to service, she is too young to work. But my husband has worn tired of paying such a sum and we quarrel all the time." She paused. "Never mind, the child is dead. I did it with a knife"' (based on press reports in Vaughan 2014).

Had the Linton Street horror started with incest? What might one do to cover it up? It shows itself as either a symptom of madness, or perhaps from the guilt, its eventual cause.

Charles Westron – *'He did not know it was wrong to kill'*

Wednesday 16 January 1856 – Murder; ?Hereditary Insanity, London
The case of Charles Westron brought several strands of debate into unsettling focus, in the years following the Rules and M'Naghten's 'escape'. His trial heard a plea for exculpatory madness – while the jury tried hard to decipher the law. More confusion arose when defence cried derangement, but prosecution counsel said he was simply depraved. So unsurprisingly vague was the eventual outcome that Justice Wightman refused to sentence the crime.

A Man's Ruin
[Note: All quotes and dialogue from *Old Bailey Proceedings Online* (see bibliography), unless otherwise stated]

On Bedford Street, London, at about half-past-ten in the morning, a solicitor's clerk, Whitfield, noted a peculiar man. His body hunched over, his spine clearly deficient, he appeared to be rummaging in the folds of his coat. At length, he set off in an easterly direction, before reaching the point where it met Bedford Row.

Whitfield watched as the man came to a standstill; followed by more sifting through pockets before he turned on his heels. But after just a few steps, he returned to the junction, and hid in the shadows of a house nearby.

Whitfield's eyes were now drawn, to a second figure approaching – as the two men drew closer, the first one spoke out: 'You villain!' he started. '[Y]ou have ruined [my fortunes]! Why! Why did you rob me?' and unbuttoned his coat.

With horror, poor Whitfield watched on as the man brought out a pistol. At the very same moment he recognised the solicitor, Waugh. The stranger pulled back on the well-oiled trigger, the crack rebounding off houses as Waugh hit the ground.

Without thinking, Whitfield raced forward; Waugh's voice was a whisper, though he heard what he said: 'Hold him … collar him … he has murdered me, [Whitfield]!'

But Whitfield just screamed: 'Why did you shoot this poor man?'

A second pistol appeared, the hammer cocked in an instant: 'He has ruined me,' he answered. 'He has robbed me of my property!'

Whitfield pointed to Waugh. 'But now you have ruined yourself!'

The stranger dismissed it. 'I don't care. I have done it!' He let the pistol fall. 'He has ruined me, now I have ruined him!'

As Waugh breathed his last, Charles Broadfoot Westron knew, then, he had murdered the man. Whether he knew it was wrong, was altogether less certain.

A Trial for the Truth

On 4 February Westron, just 25, appeared in the dock at the Old Bailey charged with murder – a hanging offence.

That he had done it, of course, was beyond any question. But it remained his counsel's position to prove he was mad. The greatest challenge he faced was his ability to reason, and his capacity to determine a right from a wrong.

Meanwhile, as a means of preventing false claims of madness, the law looked at planning and clear signs of intent. To many in court, and even the public, a crime such as this showed a rational mind…

Richard Checkley, Inspector with the (young) Metropolitan police force, announced that Westron had bought the weapons a year before. Dr Wren suggested that the shot had been practised, as the bullet had passed all the way through Waugh's heart. While James Barrell, a clerk in the late Mr Waugh's office, reported how the man was 'bound over' for making past threats.

In short, Westron's crime was no irresistible impulse (*see Part 2*); he had known it was wrong, but he shot anyway.

Westron's (Supposed) Insanity

His barrister, Ballantine, called several witnesses…

Harriet Ogborn and her husband had taken Westron as their lodger. They spoke of voluble outbursts when alone in his room. His complaints that his bed was too short for his stature were stated as proof that the man had gone mad. It was longer than him, though he still would not have it. It was enough, they insisted, to label him strange!

He would also, they added, often stand in the garden, and look back at the house every time he went out. What had offended them most was his repeated foul language – 'very bad oaths, such as [only] men use!'

As if securing his fate, Mr Ogborn then added: 'I saw him down in the kitchen' at numerous times. '[M]aking bullets [with lead] in a slice [on] the fire,' and concluded 'his conduct … was very eccentric indeed'..

Elizabeth Williams, the last witness' sister, related conversations he started and his fears of 'Old Nick'. He suggested a fire to burn out the Devil; or setting a trap to lure him outside.

She described how he liked to move the things in his bedroom; how he swore to himself as he paced up and down. 'I felt rather terrified', she confessed, and when asked for a reason, '[H]e seemed … very strange and deranged in his mind'.

Months later, Charles Essex became Westron's new landlord; at the end of the week, he ordered Westron to quit. It was, he revealed, on account of his manner, walking up and down stairs in the middle of the night.

Next, Margaret Jones said she took the man as a lodger, but after three months found him too strange to bear. When pressed for examples, she said he was too often silent, made tea in a cup [with no cover], and barked like a hound!

William Carter reported his eccentric behaviour: how he moved the things in his room while he shouted and swore. At several times, he made strange observations: like the chimney's too wide, or a keyhole too large. He reached the conclusion, if not outright crazy, he was surely a man 'not safe to be [out]'!

Elizabeth Rippon recalled one particular moment, when he upended a chair and bedecked it in clothes. A broom handle was used to create the illusion that Westron was home when in fact he was not!

Finally, Westron moved in with John Creech's mother – he had once been attendant at an asylum nearby [Grovehall]. He was used to displays of insane behaviour, and was left in no doubt the man was disturbed: 'Sometimes he would speak very rationally, at other times, perhaps in the midst of his conversation, he would break off in a very strange sort of manner'.

Under questioning, he added: 'I have sometimes noticed that he has looked very wild … I think he was at times in his right mind, but I do not think he was always'.

Madness Runs in the Family?
Hereditary insanity was a popular means of determining madness; and Ballantine used it in Westron's defence. Thomas Rodder, the family solicitor, revealed insights into Westron's own father, who had suffered a 'breakdown' before he had died.

No, he had not been confined as a lunatic patient but, yes, he did perish by cutting his throat. His brother spent two years in the local asylum and hanged himself there while alone on the ward. Their unsettled sister, Harriet Westron, had died in Brompton Asylum after years of restraint. Westron himself, the witness now added, possessed a 'morbid disposition' since being a child.

Robert Synot, a surgeon with a self-proclaimed interest, cemented the trend that the Westrons were ill. After interviewing him in Newgate, he: '... [formed] the opinion, that there was a very great deficiency of mind about [Westron] ... [T]he state of mind of the father and collateral relations is a most important feature' in a case of this sort.

He ended by addressing the right-wrong conundrum:

> 'I have heard the evidence that has been given on the subject of his father, his uncle, and one of his aunts, and I have also heard the evidence that has been given throughout the whole of this case ... [I]f all the facts deposed.. by the witnesses be true, I think the prisoner was not able to distinguish right from wrong at the time he committed the act in question.'

A Jury Confused

The presiding judge, Justice Wightman, attempted to explain to the jury the law as it stood:

> 'It is my duty to tell you that before you can come to the conclusion that the prisoner is not responsible on the ground of insanity you must be satisfied that at the time the act was committed the prisoner was labouring under such a defect of reason as not to know the nature and quality of the act he was committing' (*The Times*, 8 February 1856).

In those terms alone, Westron was doomed. The evidence against him had amounted to such.

The pre-purchase of pistols; his being bound over; his uncontrollable temper and his reasoning sense – never mind he was strange, and from a strange family. By the law of the land, he knew a right from a wrong.

The Verdict

The jury betrayed their continued confusion, when first they said 'guilty', but then added more ... prompting howls of derision, and inappropriate laughter; the foreman's oration brought farce to the court:

> 'We do not think [Westron] ought to be acquitted on the ground of insanity, but we recommend him to mercy because in his case we find there were *strong predispositions* to insanity' (in Smith 1981a: 139–40, my *emphasis*).

Whether or not Westron had known the wrong in his actions, the *possibility* of madness had proved quite enough.

This unacceptable end had left Wightman in trouble: was the verdict acquittal or guilty, corrupt or insane? He found his escape in a change to the statute … the Central Criminal Court Act several years before (1837; 1 Vict., c. 77). Now he need only *record* the death sentence, not pronounce it as fact and send the man to his death. It meant Wightman avoided the unsavoury problem, by placing the case on the Home Secretary's desk.

Reaction and concluding Remarks

Forbes Winslow, the alienist, thought the outcome unpleasant, fearing the truly insane would suffer in turn. An exculpatory verdict was not just an offence against reason, it would prove itself harmful to the alienist cause. He lambasted the verdict as 'a mockery of justice!' (in *JPM* 9: lix), and thought it a destroyer of souls and sound common sense:

> 'If capital punishment was ever justifiable, it was so in the case of [Charles] Westron,' he observed *after* the trial. 'If mere eccentricity – the use of bad language – looking up a chimney in a mysterious manner – having one or two relatives insane, are to be considered by medical men as scientific and conclusive evidence of lunacy, then the plea of insanity should be altogether abolished' (*ibid*: lvii–lx).

And this from one of its fiercest fans!

Bucknill, however, agreed with the jury's decision – that is, 'a *strong disposition* … to mental disease'. Such a thing could belie the 'actual existence of [an] insanity [condition] … incapable of proof' by regular means. Then added: '[I]mpelled to crime by a disease of the brain.. imposed upon him [despite] his *free will*' (*JMS* 2: 391–92, my *emphasis*).

In popular terms, *The Times* led the revulsion:

> 'As far as the jury are concerned, they should have either had the courage to acquit, or the firmness to condemn. As it is, here is an easy loophole of escape provided for the qualms and scruples of jurymen' (8 February 1856).

And concluded:

> 'In our opinion, nothing can be a greater mockery of all the solemnities of
> justice than the conclusion of this trial' (*ibid*).

Nonetheless, Westron's sentence was duly commuted through the Home Secretary's Mercy, who still handed down penal servitude for life. Yet, as frequently happened, his genuine madness soon showed itself beyond reasonable doubt. On 19 June, he was transferred to Bethlem Hospital, where he eventually died in July 1863.

Edward Yates & Henry Parkes – *No Victim, No Crime?*

Monday 20–Tuesday 21 October 1851 – Rape And Assault With Intent To Ravish; Victim Insane, Airdrie to Calderbank

In a particularly harrowing case, despite the flowery Victorian language, two men escaped hanging on the weakness of mind. Only not theirs, but their unfortunate victim's … alleged to be easy of virtue and simple of mind.

[Note: All quotes and dialogue from Shaw 1853, unless otherwise stated]

Elizabeth Smith, 18 or under, was known on the streets from two miserable points: first, from a common belief she worked the 'oldest profession'; and, second, her natural misfortune of having no mind ['*of infirm intellect*' – Shaw 1853].

Just before midnight, on 20 October, walking alone on the Calderbank path, she encountered two men [the defendants], who halted her progress – for Yates and Parkes saw something they liked. How this meeting of chance turned quickly to horror was never recorded by the time it reached court. In delicate terms, each took their pleasure, though no money changed hands and consent was denied.

At last breaking free, she ran off toward Airdrie – her mind in a mess, her body much worse. All too soon they were back and were quickly upon her; when they left her alone, she was sprawled on the floor.

Place, or Places Unknown

The old route brought them back to the south side of Airdrie, where they met with three others headed whence they had come. Sensing the risk of arrest, one or the other concocted a story, and one or the other implored them to wait.

'Don't go that way – there's a man nearly murdered!' They'd be back in a moment, with the local police.

Taking the men at their word, the other three waited; when the defendants returned they were still by themselves. The police would not come, they said with a saunter; the impertinent fellow said it was outside his patch! So all five agreed to go ahead slowly – they could attend to the victim then hasten for help.

As they neared the spot amidst the coalfields of Gartlee, the devious pair brought the group to a halt. It was here they had 'seen' the unfortunate victim –

by the lodge used by miners escaping the blasts. To their feigned disbelief, there was no longer a body, no signs of a struggle nor something amiss. Suggesting the man might well have recovered, the three men went looking as the two fell behind. When out of the shadows came a dissolute figure – a woman later described 'as if she [was] dead'.

The men were astounded, as each step brought her closer – she was completely uncovered, her clothes disarrayed. Had their 'nearly dead' victim been, in fact, this poor woman? Had the others not seen her and offered to help?

Elizabeth Smith, trying to recover her virtue, flung herself at the men and slumped to the floor. Looking into the dark, she saw the defendants approaching. 'Save me [from them]!' Her panic was real. And well that it was, as her attackers lunged forward, took hold of the girl and dragged her down to the floor.

Between them, the three others concocted a 'rescue' – she would be 'safer' back there, in the lodge they had passed. Whether fearful or stupid time does not mention, but they left her inside and went on their way.

They had barely gone yards when screams pierced their hearing. The hideous brutes were at it again. Returning at pace, they fought off the delinquents, and this time led Smith to the safety of town. It was now up to her, if she wished to press charges. But who around there would put trust in her word? A 'half-witted whore' was no reliable witness: easy of virtue and simple of mind.

The Victim on Trial

Around ten the next morning, she attended the station, where she told the police she wished to make a complaint. Her clothes were 'dishevelled and torn'; she had a 'depression of spirits'; and the doctor, Fordyce, confirmed signs of a rape.

The High Court hearing in Glasgow was held the day before Christmas; Yates and Parkes were charged in particular terms. 'Rape and Assault With Intent To Ravish'; in five separate locations on the Calderbank road.

The principal witnesses were her three short-sighted saviours, who related the events as reported above. The evidence they gave, and the wounds seen by the doctor, were recorded as *de recenti** – an old legal term.

---

* Meaning 'on the basis of a statement made by the victim not long after the crime'.

But two medical witnesses brought the case into question, as they confirmed the victim was of very weak mind. Indeed, since the attack, she had sunk into madness – they had to report she was *unfit to appear*.

The defence claimed her absence made the hearing a shambles: 'We must presume,' he asserted, 'she has been kept ... from the court...' Licking his lips, he delivered his climax: 'For fear she "admitted that she gave [her] consent!"'

Fordyce, for the Crown, rebuked the idea. The three witnesses proved the events had occurred. Indeed, recalling her screams as they passed through the clearing disproved the man's nonsense as disgraceful – and wrong.

She was a whore, roared defence; she no doubt welcomed the custom. In any case, evidence must be called into doubt. Who would stand by and watch what they claimed to have happened? Yet the night sky was moonless – how could they have seen?!

He duly alleged she was not a 'competent witness'. If she is so mentally ailing, then the trial should be stopped.

Lead Justice, Lord Colonsay, addressed himself to the jury. A need to postpone was *over-ruled* by the proof.

Notwithstanding the facts, he ordered Smith to appear – just to confirm her attackers, then retire again. After this had been done, His Lordship continued – and put into words what he thought should occur. The *three* men had behaved in a most curious fashion [allowed the attack to continue], yet he was of the opinion the charge be pursued:

'If the Jury ... believed that forcible connexion had taken place, then rape was relevantly and properly charged' (Shaw 1853: 531–32).

Adding:

'[W]*hatever the character of the girl*' (Shaw 1853: 531–32, my *emphasis*).

Nonetheless, he insisted they exercise caution. The victim was clearly insane and there was doubt what occurred:

'[L]ooking at her proved[?] character, the uncertainty of vision in the darkness of the night, the extraordinary conduct of the witnesses … and also the fact, that the Court and the Jury had no opportunity of knowing from the girl herself the real state of matters, the safest course for the Jury …' he thought; 'was to find assault with intent' (*ibid*: 532).

With reminders of Cruse (*see Part 5*), the jury voiced their agreement. Yates and Parkes were found guilty and sentenced at once. Each received eighteen months hard labour in gaol – to be spent in the general prison at Perth.

Afterwords

Though an odd case in manner, it raises two questions. Should the trial have been paused till the *victim* was 'sane'? And why was her 'madness' not part of the hearing as it was when the *accused* was 'unfit to stand trial'?

Appendix 1

List of Statutes

The following relevant Acts all affected the crime and insanity debates:

Date	Regnal year and chapter	Title and/or [Subject]	Key (Relevant) Impact
1800	40 Geo. III, c. 94	An Act for the Safe Custody of insane Persons charged with Offences (aka 'The Criminal Lunatics Act')	Those found 'not guilty on the ground of insanity' to be detained at His Majesty's Pleasure
1808	48 Geo. III, c. 96	The County Asylums Act	Criminal lunatics sent to Bethlem or other *mad-house*, or gaol
1832	2 & 3 Will. IV, c. 75	Anatomy Act	Ended anatomical dissection of hanged criminals
1837	1 Vict., c. 77	The Central Criminal Court Act	Home Secretary (ie not the young queen) given power of Mercy. Judges allowed to *record* the death penalty in cases of troublesome verdicts
1840	3 & 4 Vict., c. 54	The Insane Prisoners Act	Allowed incarceration of those found insane (the guilty before sentence, the accused before trial)
1842	5 & 6 Vict., c. 51	The Treason Act	Introduced 'High Misdemeanour' for lesser offences (eg no means to cause genuine harm)
1845	8 & 9 Vict., c. 100	The Lunatics Care and Treatment Act	Established Commissioners in Lunacy and certification procedures
1845	8 & 9 Vict., c. 126	The Lunatic Asylums Act	Made county asylums compulsory for pauper lunacy care

Date	Regnal year and chapter	Title and/or [Subject]	Key (Relevant) Impact
1860	23 & 24 Vict., c. 75	The Criminal Lunatics Asylum Act	Established Broadmoor for the criminally insane (opened 1863)
1861	24 & 25 Vict., c. 100	The Offences against the Person Act	Illegalised concealment through the disposal of body, whether death had occurred before, during or after the birth.
1864	27 & 28 Vict., c. 29	The Insane Prisoners Amendment Act	Tightened certification procedure and the Home Secretary's role
1865	28 & 29 Vict., c. 126	The Prison Act	Formalised medical inspection on admittance to gaol
1883	46 & 47 Vict., c. 38	The Trial of Lunatics Act	Semantic change in the verdict to 'Guilty but Insane', after attacks on the queen
1884	47 & 48 Vict., c. 64	The Criminal Lunatics Act	Amended certification procedures including for commutations of sentence

Appendix 2

Selected Key Events

Key events (*featured within*) that helped shape the crime and insanity subject:

Date	Key Event
1800	Acquittal of James Hadfield and the post-verdict Act confining dangerous lunatics
1832	Anatomy Act (2 & 3 Will. IV, c. 75) ended practice of anatomical dissection on executed criminals – most now buried within prison grounds
1837	Judges can *record* the death penalty, leaving the Home Secretary to decide on its implementation. Many cases now led to the commutation of sentence.
c.1840	Capital offences reduced from nearly 300 to just three: murder, attempted murder and treason
1843	Trial of Daniel M'Naghten and formulating 'the Rules' – 're-defining' the 'right-wrong test'
1849	Fisherton House becomes main criminal lunatic asylum after Bethlem
1861	Judges no longer allowed to *record* the death penalty – except in cases of treason, arson of the royal dockyards and armed piracy (Walker 1968: 205)
1863	Broadmoor Criminal Lunatic Asylum at Crowthorne in Berkshire opens as the new state 'repository' in Britain – first for female inmates then men nine months later
1868	Hanging in public abolished; thereafter only to take place behind prison walls

Appendix 3

The Rules

The Rules established an unwritten test of insanity in Victorian law; re-defining the vague **'right-wrong test'** (*see Glossary*) and dismissing irresistible impulse (Smith 1981a: 16). Their demand for delusions to constitute madness undermined alienist attempts with the insanity plea.

In truth, they were answers to the following confused set of questions – raised by a number of Lords concerned at M'Naghten's 'escape' (*see Part 3*). Not everybody took part – Justice Maule was a critic – their general tone made them balefully vague (see Smith 1981a: 15).

All *emphasis* my own:

1. What is the law respecting alleged crimes committed by persons afflicted with *insane delusion*, in respect of one or more particular subjects or persons: as, for instance, where at the time of the commission of the alleged crime, *the accused knew he was acting contrary to the law*, but did the act complained of with a view, under the influence of an insane delusion, of redressing or revenging some supposed grievance or injury, or of producing some supposed public benefit?
2. What are the proper questions to be submitted to the jury, when a person alleged to be afflicted with *insane delusion* respecting one or more particular subjects or persons, is charged with the commission of a crime (murder, for example), and *insanity is set up as a defence?*
3. In what terms ought the question to be left to the jury, as to the *prisoner's state of mind* at the time when the act was committed?
4. If a person under an *insane delusion* as to existing facts, commits and offence in consequence thereof, is he thereby excused?
5. Can a *medical man* conversant with the *disease of insanity*, who never saw the prisoner previously to the trial, but who was present during the whole trial and the examination of all the witnesses, be asked his opinion as to the *state of the prisoner's mind* at the time of the commission of the alleged crime, or hi opinion whether the prisoner was *conscious at the time of doing the act, that he was acting contrary to the law*, or whether he was labouring under any and what *delusion* at the time?

(after Walker 1968: 97)

Appendix 4

Early Forensics

Two accounts of early forensic toxicology in cases of murder (see Part 5):

Dr Letheby's explanation of his analysis of arsenic, as given at Allnutt's Old Bailey trial, 1847

'I used tests of my own, which are known only to a few. They are known tests, but somewhat modified. I can state that there was not any material used that contained arsenic, inasmuch as experiments were performed with portions of sheep's liver, and so on, which did not yield to the same reagents any indication of arsenic.

The contents of the stomach were first put into a retort and distilled, and about three tea-spoonsful of liquor distilled from it. Those three tea-spoonsful were tested for prussic acid, without giving any evidence or indication of that poison. The remainder of the contents of the stomach were evaporated nearly to dryness, then digested in about half a pint of alcohol, then about half a pint of alcohol poured upon this nearly dry deposit. This alcoholic solution was then filtered, and then tested for lead, corrosive sublimate, copper, and beryta, all of which are poisons; also for opium, *nux vomica* and oxalic acid, but without being able to detect either of them.

The remainder of the contents of the stomach not dissolved by the alcohol was then boiled in water and tested for arsenic, by which means I was enables (*sic*) to detect that poison, a portion of which I produce in a metallic state. It is the small metallic ring in this tube (*produced*) that is only a portion of what I discovered; the other has been subjected to analysis. The liver was then tested for arsenic, and that gave similar results. I then proceeded to analyse the arrow-root, but did not detect any poison there. I then analysed the coarse white sugar, which amounted to four ounces and a half, and out of that I was enabled to obtain this, which is rather more than half an ounce of white arsenic. I afterwards examined a portion of the brain, which was given me by Mr Toulmin three of four days afterwards, I cannot remember the day, it was at one of the sitting of the Coroner's Jury. I analysed that, and detected a trace of arsenic in the brain.

I did not weigh the quantity of arsenic I found in the stomach, but in my judgment I should say I detected about four grains of white arsenic in the stomach, liver, intestines, and brain altogether. I weighed one portion, and from that obtained rather better than two grains and a half, nearly three grains, of white arsenic in the intestines. I think that would be sufficient to cause death.

I can form an opinion, from discovering arsenic in the liver, how long the patient had been under its influence. I may be wrong, but I am of opinion that the deceased had been under the influence of arsenic of few days. I am speaking from my experience in similar cases. From the time it takes to get arsenic into the system, I think he must have had it in him for about a week. That which was contained in the intestines might have been taken recently. I should say he had taken it very recently before death. In my judgment the arsenic was the cause of death.'

Transcribed from *Old Bailey Proceedings Online*: trial of William Newton Allnutt (t18471213-290)

* * *

Mr Overend QC, outlining the effects of strychnia (strychnine) to the jury in Dove's case, 1856

'Gentlemen, It may be useful if I describe to you the kind of poison which has been used in this case – what is its nature, what its operation, and what are its effects. The poison which, it is suggested on the part of the prosecution, was used by the prisoner, is the poison known as strychnia; and, unfortunately, strychnia is a poison which has been much talked of by the public.

It is a vegetable poison, and extracted by chemical agency from a plant called *Strychnot* (*sic*) which bears a nut or bean known as *nux vomica*. The poison is extracted from the bark or root of the plant; and from a quarter to three-quarters of a grain has been known to destroy life. A grain and a half is what medical gentlemen would call a full dose; therefore you see that a very small portion of this poison is enough to take away the life of an individual.

It is very bitter: and this is a matter you will have to bear carefully in mind; for what is suggested by the prosecution is that it was administered in some medicine which was taken by the victim; and therefore the taste would be as apparent as the effects. It is, then, exceedingly and intensely bitter to the taste, which you will perhaps bear in mind. It is nearly insoluble in water; easily soluble in acids; and insoluble in alkalies (*sic*).

The period when it begins to take effect is from a quarter of an hour to an hour. This depends on the amount given, and the vehicle in which it is conveyed-whether in a soluble (or fluid) state or in a solid form – whether there is much food in the stomach – whether the party receiving it has great powers of absorption – or whether the contents of the stomach by which it is received are acid or alkaloid in character. If alkaloid, the poison would be difficult to dissolve; if acid, then it would dissolve very easily. Therefore, you will perceive that the poison will operate sooner or later, according to the state of the stomach, the condition of the person taking it, the vehicle by which it is administered, and the form in which it is when passed into the stomach.

After the first effect of the poison is felt, its continuance varies from half an hour to two or three hours, according to the state of the patient, and whether the dose is sufficient to produce a fatal result.

The operation of the poison is this: it is absorbed into the system, passed into the blood, and circulates throughout the whole frame; but its great and principal effect is on the spine and spinal marrow. The muscles of the body are peculiarly affected; the muscles of the touch – the grasping muscles – are affected in a very remarkable manner. All the nerves of sensation are peculiarly affected; and there is this very remarkable peculiarity that all the nerves which the organ of intelligence, the brain, are unaffected by it. So that while there are great spasms of the muscles, great contractions of some portions, and paroxysms almost beyond endurance, the consciousness of the mind remains, and the patient is well aware of what is going on. This is the great peculiarity of this poison, and differs materially from opium, which acts upon the brain and produces insensibility almost immediately after it is taken.

There is another peculiarity in the poison strychnine. It is not a cumulative poison. If you give a patient a mineral poison, like arsenic, in a very small quantity, it will produce very little effect; if you give more, it will produce a greater effect; and so on with every repetition of the dose, until you produce the most dreadful effects, and eventually death. But this is not the case with strychnia. It is not a cumulative poison. As it passes through the system it produces a certain effect at once upon the kidneys, spleen, and lungs; but if the dose be too small to destroy life, it loses all power, and passes away from the system.

If the effect upon the patient is not speedily fatal, although the effects are very painful, especially during the worst paroxysms, the whole effect passes off, and the patient is left almost without any ill effects, except the exhaustion which must ensue from the paroxysms, and the unnatural strain upon the muscles and nerves of the body. There however, is no remainder left behind; nothing by which a second dose of the same quantity would act with greater effect; nothing which would act in the way of cumulation, as is arsenic and most mineral poisons.

There are peculiar and remarkable symptoms of poisoning by strychnine. At first the patient is affected with spasms or jerkings of the extremities; the hands are clenched; the muscles of the arms and legs are convulsed; then the legs and arms are jerked; then there is a difficulty of respiration, and painful efforts to get breath, the reason of which is, that, as the doctors will tell you, the poison fixes the lungs, which are unable to act, and if the paroxysm continues long enough, then death ensues from suffocation.

The first effect is upon the extremities of the legs and hands; and the next is its operation upon the back of the neck and the whole spinal cord; and the body assumes a form which is peculiar to poison by strychnia and one form of disease. The body assumes the form almost of a bow; and the patient is unable to lie so that the back rests wholly upon the bed; indeed, the body becomes so arched that the patient rests upon the heels and back of the head, and when the spasms are very violent the arch of the back is so great that a pillow has to be placed under it.

From this you will form some conception of how great the agony must be of those who are poisoned by strychnine. After this effect upon the arms, the back, and the difficulty of respiration, the next thing is the difficulty of swallowing or opening the mouth, and the spasmodic action of the jaws. And there is also dilation of the eyes, and a peculiar expression of the face which once seen is never forgotten. This sometimes continues till death, and with slight interruption till the last paroxysm.

Death is caused in one of two ways. By the muscles fixing the lungs, and thus producing apoplexy. Or else by causing great exhaustion, under which the patient sinks. When the attack is not fatal the symptoms are the same, but their intensity is less, and they do not continue over a certain time, after which the patient recovers, suffering scarcely anything but great exhaustion, arising from the agony the patient has endured, and the great contraction of the muscles. The poison works itself out, and discharges itself from the system.

Now, gentlemen, these symptoms, and the order in which they proceed, are inconsistent with any known disease. But there is a certain kind of disease which in some degree resembles it. This is traumatic and idiomatic tetanus. Traumatic tetanus is produced by a wound – and a very slight wound is sometimes sufficient to produce it – by cutting the finger, for example. But the effects thus produced, though somewhat similar in appearance, do not occur in the same order as when resulting from poison by strychnia.

In strychnia it is a question of an hour; in tetanus it is one of days and weeks; in tetanus the first symptom is the locking of the jaw; in poisoning by strychnia it is the last; in tetanus the patient suffers little in the first instance, and the symptoms go on increasing till the patient expires, but in poisoning by strychnia this is not the case. These are the distinguishing features between the two cases.

Idiomatic tetanus follows the same course, and is probably called so because it arises from no known cause. It is distinguished from traumatic tetanus by not being produced by a wound. I believe it is very rare indeed in this country, though it is sometimes met with in India. I need not, however, dwell further on this matter of traumatic and idiomatic tetanus, as my learned friends on the other side will not trouble me upon the point of whether the deceased was poisoned by strychnia…

I shall prove that in the body of Mrs Dove we found a quantity of strychnia, and that the presence of this strychnia will explain all the symptoms, explain the death, and distinguish the case from traumatic or idiomatic tetanus.'

Transcribed from Williams 1856

Bibliography

Selected Primary Sources

19th Century British Newspapers – http://find.galegroup.com/bncn/ [accessed up to and including 2016 – subscription required (or via some public libraries and archives)]

Hansard – HC Deb 10 June 1856 vol 142 cols 1231–261) http://hansard.millbanksystems.com/ [accessed up to and including March 2016]

Hansard – HC Deb 20 May 1856 vol 142 col 428 http://hansard.millbanksystems.com/ [accessed up to and including March 2016]

Illustrated Police News Digital Archive – http://find.galegroup.com/ttda/ [accessed up to and including 2016 – subscription required (or via some public libraries and archives)]

Old Bailey Proceedings Online version 7.2 – Bates: t18370918-2126, t18490129-583; Turton: t18540508-631, t18550820-768; Dyer: t18960518-451; Allnutt: t18471213-290; Brixey: t18450512-1180; Sommer: t18560407-457; Westron: t18560204-263; Parnell: t18510106-384, t18510203-546 http://www.oldbaileyonline.org [accessed up to and including March 2016]

The Times Digital Archive – http://find.galegroup.com/ttda/ [accessed up to and including March 2016 – subscription required (or via some public libraries and archives)]

(WSHC) Wiltshire and Swindon History Centre archives

Selected Secondary Sources

(C&K) *Carrington & Kirwan Reports*, Nisi Prius

(C&P) *Carrington and Payne's Reports*, Nisi Prius

(Couper) Couper, C. T. (1871–1887), *Reports of Cases Before the High Court and Circuit Courts of Justiciary in Scotland*, Edinburgh: Clark

(Cox C C) Cox, E. W. (1843–1945), *Reports of Cases in Criminal Law Argued and Determined in all the Courts in England and Ireland*, 30 vols, London: J. Crockford and others

(EMSJ) *Edinburgh Medical and Surgical Journal*

(ER) *The English Reports* (1900–1930), 176 vols, Edinburgh: Green

(HMSO) Her Majesty's Stationery Office 1868, *Report of the Capital Punishment Commission; together with the minutes of evidence and appendix*, Sydney: Thomas Richards

(HMSO) Her Majesty's Stationery Office 1866, *Report of the Capital Punishment Commission; together with the minutes of evidence and appendix*, London

(IPN) *Illustrated Police News*

(JMS) *[Asylum] Journal of Mental Science*

(JPM) *Journal of Psychological Medicine and Mental Pathology*

(LMG) *London Medical Gazette*, new series

Shaw, J. 1853, *Reports of Cases Before the High Court and Circuit Courts of Justiciary in Scotland*, Edinburgh: Clark

Bibliography

A Prison Matron 1862, *Female Life in Prison* (Vols. 1, 2), London: Hurst and Blackett

Bousfield, R. M. and R. Merrett 1843, *Report of the Trial of Daniel M'Naughton*, London: Henry Renshaw

Brown, A. 2013, Social History of Scottish Homicide, 1836–69, published PhD thesis

Bucknill, J. C. & D. H. Tuke 1858, *A Manual Of Psychological Medicine*, Philadelphia: Blanchard and Lea

Bucknill, J. C. (?) 1857, Plea Of Insanity – The Trial Of William Dove, *Asylum JMS* 3, 125–34

Bucknill, J. C. 1857 *Unsoundness Of Mind In Relation To Criminal Acts*, London: Longman, Brown, Green, Longmans and Roberts

Bucknill, J. C. 1856, Criminal Jurisprudence of Insanity, *Asylum JMS* 2, 391–92

Combe, A 1831, *Observations on Mental Derangement: being an Application of the Principles of Phrenology to the Elucidation of the Causes, Symptoms, Nature, and Treatment of Insanity*, Edinburgh: John Anderson

Cowles Prichard, J. 1822, *Treatise on Diseases of the Nervous System*, London: T. & G. Greenwood

Darby, R. 2003, The masturbation taboo and the rise of routine male circumcision: A review of the historiography, *Journal of Social History* 27, 737–57

Davey, J. G. 1860, A Case of Homicidal Mania, *JMS* 7, 49–59

Davies, O. 2005, *Murder, magic, madness. The Victorian trials of Dove and the Wizard* London: Longman

Dymond, A. H. 1865, *The Law on its trial: or, personal recollections of the death penalty and its opponents*, London: Alfred W. Bennett

Eign, J. P. 2003, *Unconscious Crime: Mental Absence and Criminal Responsibility in Victorian London*, London: The John Hopkins University Press

Esquirol, E. (tr. E. K. Hunt) 1845, *Mental maladies. A treatise on insanity*, Philadelphia: Lea and Blanchard

Fraser's Magazine 51 (1855), 'Moral Insanity – Dr Mayo's Croonian Lectures', 245–59

Gibbs, R. 1878–1882, *Buckinghamshire a Record of Local Occurrences and General Events, Chronologically Arranged* (4 vols.), Aylesbury

Goodman, H. 2015, Madness and Masculinity': Male Patients in London Asylums and Victorian Culture. In Knowles, T. and S. Trowbridge (eds.), *Insanity and the Lunatic Asylum in the Nineteenth Century*, London: Pickering & Chatto

Green, A. and K. Troup (eds.), *The Houses of History. A Critical Reader in Twentieth Century History and Theory*, Manchester: University Press

Laycock, T. 1845, 'On the reflex function of the brain'. In *The British and Foreign Medical Review* **19**: **298–311**

Laycock, T. 1840, *A Treatise on the Nervous Diseases of Women: Comprising an Inquiry Into the Nature, Causes, and Treatment of Spinal and Hysterical Disorders*, London: Longman, Orme, Brown, Green, and Longmans

Lockhart Robertson, C. 1847, The Consciousness of Right and Wrong a just test of partial insanity in criminal cases, *Edinburgh Medical and Surgical Journal* 68, 156–72

Lord Cockburn 1889, *Circuit Journeys*, Edinburgh: David Douglas

Maudsley, H. 1896 (1874), *Responsibility in Mental Disease*, New York: D. Appleton

Maudsley, H. 1874, Sex in Mind and in Education, *Fortnightly Review* 15, 466–83

Mayo, T. 1865, On The Liabilities Of Criminal Lunatics, *British Medical Journal* (2/242), 180

Mayo, T. 1847, *Clinical Facts and Reflections: also Remarks on the Impunity of Murder in some Cases of Presumed Insanity*, London: Longman, Brown, Green and Longmans

Morison, A. 1848 (1825), *Outlines of Lectures on the Natures, Causes and Treatment of Insanity*, London: Longman, Brown, Green and Longmans

Morison, A. 1843, *The Physiognomy of Mental Diseases*, London: Longman and Company

Oates, J. 2012, *Buckinghamshire Murders*, Stroud: The History Press

Prichard, J. C. 1837 (1835), *A Treatise on Insanity and Other Disorders Affecting the Mind*, Philadelphia: E. L. Carey and A. Hart

Prichard, J. C. 1822, *A Treatise on Diseases of the Nervous System*, London: T. & G. Underwood

Rattle, A. & A. Vale 2007, *Amelia Dyer: Angel Maker: The Woman Who Murdered Babies for Money*, London: Andre Deutsch

Ray, I. 1838, *A Treatise on the Medical Jurisprudence of Insanity*, Boston: Charles C. Little And James Brown

Scull, A. 2011, *Madness. A Very Short Introduction*, Oxford: University Press

Shepherd, A. 2015, *Institutionalizing the Insane in Nineteenth-Century England*, London: Pickering and Chatto

Showalter, E. 1987 (1985), *The Female Malady. Women, Madness and English Culture, 1830–1980*, London: Virago Press

Smith, R. 1981a, *Trial by Medicine. Insanity and Responsibility in Victorian Trials*, Edinburgh: University Press

Smith, R. 1981b, The Boundary between insanity and criminal responsibility in 19th century England. In Scull (ed.), *Madhouses, mad-doctors, and madmen: the social history of psychiatry in the Victorian era*, London: The Athlone Press, 363–84

The Spectator [see http://archive.spectator.co.uk/ (accessed up to and including March 2016)]

Stephen, J. F. 1883, *A History of the Criminal Law of England*, 3 vols, London: R. Clay, Sons and Taylor

Taylor, A.S. 1873(1865), *Principles and Practice of Medical Jurisprudence* vol. 2, 2nd edn., Philadelphia: Henry C. Lea

Taylor, A.S. 1865, *Principles and Practice of Medical Jurisprudence*, London: John Churchill & Sons

Tuke, D. H. 1891, *Prichard and Symonds. In Especial Relation to Mental Science. With Chapters on Moral Insanity*, London: J & A Churchill

Tuke, D. H. 1884, *Sleep-Walking and Hypnotism*, London: Churchill

Tuke, D. H. 1882, *Chapters in the History of the Insane in the British Isles*, London: Kegan Paul, Trench & Co

van Whye, J. n.d., http://www.historyofphrenology.org.uk/davey.html [accessed January 2016]

Vaughan, D. J. 2014, The Secret Life of Celestina Sommer. A very Victorian Murder http://www.amazon.co.uk/Secret-Life-Celestina-Sommer-Victorian-ebook/dp/B00J2ERTM2

Walker, N. 1968, *Crime and Insanity in England. Vol. One: The Historical Perspective*, Edinburgh: University Press

Walkowitz, J. R. 1994 (1992), *City of Dreadful Delight. Narratives of Sexual Danger in Late-Victorian London*, London: Virago Press

Williams, C. 1856, *Observations On The Criminal Responsibility Of The Insane: Founded On The Trials Of James Hill And William Dove*, London: John Churchill

Winslow, F. 1843, *The Plea of Insanity in Criminal Cases*, Boston: Charles C. Little And James Brown

Winslow, F. 1842, *On the Preservation of the Health of Body and Mind*, London: Henry Renshaw

Winslow F. 1840, *The Anatomy of Suicide*, London: Henry Renshaw

Online

Anatomy at Edinburgh http://www.ed.ac.uk/biomedical-sciences/anatomy/anatomy museum/exhibits/howison [accessed September 2015]

Ancestry including England Censuses, Criminal Register, Criminal Lunatic Register, UK Lunacy Patients Admission Registers, Criminal Lunatic Asylum Registers, London Workhouse Admission and Discharge Records, Australian Convict Transportation Registers, etc http://ancestry.com [accessed up to and including 2016]

Andrew Roberts website "specialising in social science and mental health history" http://studymore.org.uk/ [accessed up to and including 2016]

English Broadside Ballad Archive http://ebba.english.ucsb.edu/ [accessed January 2016]

Gale Digital Collections http://www.gdc.gale.com [accessed up to and including March 2016]

Monklands Memories http://www.monklands.co.uk/airdrie/airdriehouse.htm [accessed up to and including March 2016]

(Oxford DNB) *Oxford Dictionary of National Biography*, http://www.oxforddnb.com [accessed up to and including 2016 – subscription required (or via some public libraries and archives)]

(OED) *Oxford Dictionary Online* http://www.oxforddictionaries.com [accessed up to and including March 2016]

Thames Valley Police Museum http://www.thamesvalley.police.uk/ [accessed January 2016]

Wiltshire Online Parish Clerks (OPCs) http://www.wiltshire-opc.org.uk/Items/Fisherton%20Anger/Fisherton%20Anger%20-%20Murder%20of%20Mary%20Kenney%201858.pdf [accessed April 2016]

Index